Creating Sensory Play at Little or No Cost

Using everyday resources

written by
Wendy Usher
The Play Doctors

Contents

Sensory play encourages children to learn, laugh, have fun and participate. Use the activities in this book to help develop your own ideas and to encourage children to use their own imagination. Let the children guide you in relation to their play, and enjoy sitting back and seeing how their play develops. Our role as adults is to enhance and enable play. Don't be tempted to take over.

Most importantly, enjoy yourself and have fun!

Wendy Usher

We have suggested ideas for activities for the following age groups.

When you see this sign, the activity is appropriate to all ages, including babies. Be aware that for some children their developmental stage is younger than their chronological age. Adapt each activity according to the ability of the individual.

When you see these signs, the activities are suitable for Early Years (EY ages 2-4) and Primary Plus (P+ ages 5 and upwards). Activities may be adapted for older children; look out for extension activity ideas.

The book illustrates learning points using short case studies appearing in purple boxes or in purple text.

We would like to thank the children who were willing to be photographed for the illustrations throughout this book – especially Nyasha and Rutendo Chikore, who appear in many of the books that Grandma writes! Further practical resource books written by Wendy Usher are published by The Play Doctors (www.theplaydoctors.co.uk).

We also thank Widgit Symbols, who have allowed us to use their symbols within the book.

©Widgit Software 2002-2013 (www.widgit.com).

When we think of our senses we tend to consider the five obvious ones: sight, sound, taste, touch and smell.

However, our sensory world is far more than this. What about the sense of fairness, having a sense of judgement or just plain old common sense!

In this book we are going to concentrate on seven senses and will be using the ©Widgit symbols below to illustrate what sense we are concentrating on in each suggested activity. Many activities involve more than one sense.

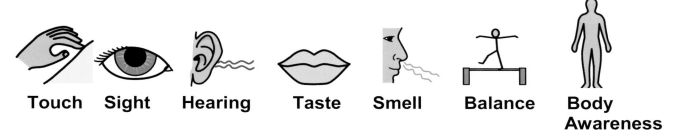

Touch   Sight   Hearing   Taste   Smell   Balance   Body Awareness

The majority of children love sensory play and enjoy using their senses to enhance their play experiences. However, some children have sensory integration difficulties, which can affect how the child or young person responds to sensory stimuli and to other people.

Think about sensory stimuli from your own perspective. Do you have any particular aversions? Perhaps you dislike the sound of fingernails being scraped down a blackboard, or have sensitivity to strobe lights and would prefer to stay away from these experiences. Respect the choices of the child and understand that they too will have their own response to sensory play.

Throughout this book we provide a wide range of ideas offering activities to enhance the sensory experiences for all children and young people. It is important to know the child or young person you are playing with and to understand what sensitivities they may have in order to ensure that the activity is appropriate. This will be different for each child. When introducing sensory play, consider the activity from a person-centred approach. We encourage risk in play, but always be aware that some activities require supervision, child safety is paramount and remains your responsibility.

Sensory play does not need to take place in a designated area or sensory room. We are surrounded by opportunities to encourage sensory play every day. In fact, all play has an element of sensory stimulation.

Just for a moment, stop reading this book and consider your environment. Are you aware of heat, cold, light, the chair you are sitting on, the proximity of someone near you? All of these environmental inputs are helping us to make sense of the world around us.

We all interpret senses in different ways and to different degrees. Consider how you can adapt the ideas suggested to break down any barriers to participation and to ensure that all the activities are inclusive.

So, how do our senses work and how is it different for each individual?
Our brains process sensory information and sensory stimuli through receptors all over the body, for example, we feel 'touch' through our skin, especially our hands and feet. We process the information automatically and our brain then responds through thoughts, feelings or behavioural responses.

If you were to touch a hot surface, before you have time to register the sensation the brain has processed the information and your body pulls your hand away from the heat source. The brain has registered potential danger and your body releases adrenaline and reacts.

People with sensory sensitivities and/or sensory integration difficulties do not process everyday sensory information in the same way. They may exhibit different types of responses, some of which may be unexpected, including the lack of pain or understanding danger.

Others may be more susceptible and feel physical pain to simple stimuli such as touch. This may result in unusual or difficult behaviour. Some may find sensory stimuli stressful and become over anxious, illustrating this through their behaviour.

Behaviour itself is a form of communication. If this is so, then what is the communication behind the behaviour telling you? Be aware of the individual child or young person, and keep checking their responses to new activities.

 Joanne does not like having baths or going swimming. She pulls back from the sensation of water, screaming and shouting. She even dislikes washing her hands.

While away on holiday, the cottage the family were staying in did not have a bath but had a power shower.

The shower was left on full power, and Joanne's parents did not realise this. When Joanne stepped into the shower and experienced the sensation of powerful water jets hitting her body, she stopped crying, stood still and enjoyed the sensation, allowing her mum to wash her.

Her parents then realised that Joanne hated the sensation of still or slow running water but could enjoy a powerful jet. It was nothing to do with the water itself or the temperature but how the water was touching her.

Some people have difficulty in coping with too many senses at any one time. One young lady who is sensitive to noise described it as listening to twenty radio stations at the same time and not being able to distinguish one from another.

Some individuals may have had a diagnosis of sensory integration disorder (SID) or sensory processing disorder (SPD). It is rare that this is diagnosed on its own;it is often as a dual diagnosis along with autism, dyspraxia or other conditions. Often, it remains undiagnosed, but traits of SID/SPD are easily seen from the child's responses to sensory stimuli.

 There are two different kinds of sensitivities: hypo (under-sensitive) and hyper (over-sensitive). The following pages provide a rough guide to how individuals may experience the world around them. Remember that each person is an individual, and not all people will experience the same things.

When working with someone who has SID/SPD or who may find sensory play difficult, keep a note of the child's reactions. Remember to pass this information on to others. If the child is unable to communicate, take photographs to remind yourself of positive and negative activities.

During a summer play scheme, Tim, a play worker, asked John, who has a learning disability and no verbal communication, if he would like to play with musical instruments.

While participating in the activity, the young man covered his ears and started to sway backwards and forwards. He was demonstrating that he found the situation too noisy, so Tim took him elsewhere in the setting.

The following day, Tim was not in, so another team member supported John. He suggested that John might like to join in music making. Again, John covered his ears and this time started to cry.

No message had been left to say that John was sensitive to noise. He had been put in an uncomfortable position because communication between staff was poor.

Later in the week, Tim picked up a tambourine and helped John to make sounds. In isolation, with just one instrument, John enjoyed making music. He could not cope with lots of sound at the same time. Tim wrote this down in the communication book to be passed on to other staff members.

SID and SPD are neurological disorders that result from the brain's inability to process and respond to sensory stimuli. Normally, the brain will process the information provided from all the senses and respond accordingly. This process is called sensory integration and enables us to make sense of the world around us.

If the process is disrupted, the brain does not receive messages, messages are received inconsistently or the messages may not connect properly so the receiver only gets part of the picture.

The disorder impacts people's lives in different ways. Some signs may include:

- Hyper or hyposensitivity to touch, movements, sights, smells, taste or sounds
- Particularly high or low activity levels
- Difficulty with transition – making the change from one situation to another
- Difficulty in concentration, easily distracted, limited attention
- Social/emotional difficulties
- Impulsiveness
- Difficulty in reasoning (lack of self-control, inability to unwind or calm down)
- Being clumsy or uncoordinated

These are just a few of the possible signs of SID/SPD.

Children may also have difficulty with managing anxiety, self managing stressful situations, dealing with frustration, staying on task, self-organisation or effectively using fine and gross motor skills.

SID/SPD is linked closely to social communication impairments, including autism. Children may not respond as expected to sensory stimuli or may be uninterested in sensory experiences. Others may be hypersensitive, responding negatively to noise, crowds, bright colours and new situations.

Some children may not experience the same sensations we feel, for example, feeling hot or cold or feeling the need to go to the toilet.

Individuals may use a range of behaviour to cope with SID/SPD, including fight or flight. Some children may fight against stimulation by overreacting emotionally; others may want to run away or hide.

Some children are able to manage the impairment by putting their hands over their ears, or they take part in distraction activities such as flapping hands or spinning.

Occupational therapists (OTs) can support children by providing sensory integration therapy. After assessment, a specifically designed suite of activities is suggested for each individual child, taking a person-centred approach.

Jhasinda happens to have autism and dyspraxia. When she was young she hated light touch, stroking her skin was painful for her and she would pull away. She would not keep any covers on in bed and hated 'light' clothes. She needed a very firm pressure to help her feel comfortable.

The OT taught her parents to play a game using therapeutic body brushing, simply using a wallpaper brush applied firmly across her arms and legs. They were also advised to wrap her tightly in a soft blanket and play rough and tumble by rolling her across the floor.

This was done for a few minutes several times a day gradually reducing the pressure until she began to respond more appropriately to a lighter touch.

The most important step is for adults to recognise behaviour that may be associated with SID/SPD. It does exist and the children are not just 'being silly' or 'naughty' in relation to their responses to sensory stimuli.

Take a child-centred approach and put yourself into their shoes. Think about how you can adapt your own behaviour and their environment or activities in order to support SID/SPD.

The next few pages explore how individuals who are hypo or hypersensitive may respond to sensory stimuli.

Touch

 We all know what type of touch we feel comfortable with, especially touch that gives the feeling of comfort and being safe. This is different for each individual: perhaps being in a warm bath, or snuggling under blankets.

Human touch is the basic foundation for social development and helps us to build our social skills. Touch helps us assess the environment and increases our understanding of how to react.

Hyposensitivity to touch may mean that an individual craves for the sensation of being touched, but may not recognise how much pressure to give when holding or touching others.

This may mean that the child constantly gives 'bear hugs'. They may have a very high pain threshold and may not recognise the pain associated with an injury. Some children will enjoy extremes, for example, rubbing sand over their arms or having very hot/cold baths. Some children benefit from the use of weighted blankets and find them very comforting. This is described in more detail later in the book.

Ben, who happens to be on the autism spectrum, once saw his Mum scald her arm. He was fascinated with her burn blisters. She gave him clear instructions that he should not go near the kettle.

Later in the day, Ben decided he wanted blisters too, so he boiled the kettle and poured the water over his own arm. He did not feel any pain, but was happy to show his mum he had similar blisters!

Hypersensitivity may mean that individuals do not like being touched, finding it uncomfortable or even painful. This can affect their social skills and relationships. Some children will not recognise spatial awareness and will stand too close to others, but will strike out if others come too close to them.

Some children do not like the sensation of clothes, preferring to be naked, or will only wear particular textures such as soft, loose cotton. Others dislike having their hair brushed or washed or wearing shoes. The ways in which this presents is different for each child.

Sight

 We use variations in light to help define contrast, objects, colours, people and spatial boundaries. Some people may see things in different ways.

For someone who is **hyposensitive**, objects may appear darker or be less defined. Central vision may be blurred but peripheral vision good, or the other way round, where central vision is good but peripheral is poor. People may experience a poor depth of vision perception, resulting in clumsiness and misjudging space and placement.

 Individuals who are **hypersensitive** may have distorted vision. Imagine yourself looking through a kaleidoscope, where objects and bright lights seem to jump around or fragment. It is easier to focus on single detail rather than the 'whole'.

If you are living or working with a child who has visual impairment, get to know what the best approach is for that individual. Find out what colour contrasts to use and what type of lighting is appropriate.

Sound

Out of all the sensory impairments hearing is the most common and will affect how an individual communicates. Many children with significant hearing impairments will use a form of augmented communication. This may be in the form of a hearing aid, a technological solution, sign language or the use of symbol cards.

Some children with no obvious hearing impairment may still be over or undersensitive to sound. Children with **hyposensitivity** are likely to enjoy loud noises, and may constantly bang doors, shout and scream and look for opportunities to play with noisy toys. An individual may hear sounds better from one particular side. Some sounds and pitches may not be acknowledged although they are heard.

Children who are **hypersensitive** may find that sounds are muddled and distorted. One child described hearing an adult's voice as 'being in another room' as though hearing it from a distance. Another child found a ticking clock painful; the pitch of the ticking cut through all other sounds and became the focus for the child. He was unable to distinguish any other sounds apart from the ticking.

Taste

Tastes are primarily defined by receptors on our tongue. As babies, sensory experiences through the mouth are very important. Children initially search for milk, which leads on to further sensory exploration, including sucking fingers, the edge of a blanket, clothing or any objects that come into contact with their mouths.

It is through the mouth that, as babies, we determine if objects are hard or soft. Some children do not outgrow this need to explore their environment through mouthing objects. This often results in a battle when trying to stop a child from constantly putting things in their mouth. Mouthing includes the sensations of both taste and touch and is often associated with smell.

Hyposensitivity may mean that a child likes very strong tastes such as spicy food and will try to eat anything, for example, grass and washing-up liquid. **Hypersensitivity** may mean that the child dislikes any strong flavours and will choose to restrict their diet to things they can tolerate. Additionally, certain textures may cause discomfort such as crunchy foods or runny foods.

Smell

We all have preferences for smell. Out of a group of five people, three may like the smell of a particular air freshener and two can't stand it as the smell gives them a headache. This is no different for children, but they may not be able to communicate or let us know what they like or dislike.

Some people cannot smell particular fragrances such as roses or lemons. Smell is often the first sense we have of danger, for example, we may smell heat before we see the smoke and flames or may choose not to eat a particular food because it 'smells off'.

Hyposensitivity to smell may mean that people have little or no sense of smell and do not recognise extreme odours. Some children will prefer to lick things and rely on taste rather than smell. Mouthing items is very closely aligned to hyposensitivity in smell.

Hypersensitivity may mean that children find smells too intense and overpowering. Some individuals will want to smell something or someone before they interact with it. This can cause embarrassment if a child wants to come and smell you before being introduced. If the child does not like the smell of the perfume or deodorant you are using they may make a decision not to interact with you. Toileting can be an issue for some children who find the smell too intense, sometimes resulting in constipation or an unwillingness to go to the toilet.

Shauna is fascinated by smells. Her sense of smell is the strongest sense she has, overriding sight, touch or hearing. When she meets someone new for the first time she decides if she likes them by smelling them first.

Her mother has to explain to other people that she makes sense of the world by using smell. It becomes very difficult when Shauna visits supermarkets; she stops at each shelf to smell the goods before they are put into the trolley.

When queuing to pay, her mum gives her strongly smelling items to play with to prevent her from sniffing the lady waiting in front!

Balance

To maintain our balance and posture we use the vestibular system in our brains, where information has been provided from organs within the inner ear. This sensory system helps us to understand where we are in space and how fast our bodies are moving.

Have you ever spun round and round very fast and afterwards felt dizzy? Some children thoroughly enjoy this experience and spin around by themselves to feel the sensation. **Hyposensitivity** to balance often results in a need to rock backwards and forwards, swing, spin or move the body in a certain way in order to attain sensory input.

Hypersensitivity results in difficulties where we need to control our movements quickly. Children may find it difficult to stop suddenly or to change direction quickly.

Some children may have travel sickness or difficulties where the activity involves the head not being upright or where feet are off the ground (such as swinging). Others may have difficultly participating in quick action sports.

Body awareness

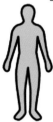

Body awareness is when our brain tells us where our body is in space and how it is moving. Children who have **hypo** body awareness may stand too close to others and have difficulty in judging personal space. They may constantly bump into objects or misjudge distances when walking through a doorway. Some children will regularly bump into people in the classroom or corridor.

Children who are **hypersensitive** may have difficulty with fine motor skills, holding a pencil, doing up a button or using a paper clip. Some children will not just turn their head to look at something but will need to turn their entire body.

Lastly, something that is very rare but can be experienced, particularly by people on the autism spectrum, is when a sensory experience is transposed from one sense to another. A person may hear a sound but experience it as a colour, so in their mind's eye a ticking clock becomes the colour purple. In other cases, people may see numbers as colours, so a maths equation results in many colours shifting and rejoining and the resulting answer is translated into a number. This is a particular form of Savant autism.

So what is sensory play?

Sensory play is any opportunity provided that enhances the use and development of our senses. This may involve all senses or may just focus on a particular one. It can involve the environment, physical space, the use of play equipment or can involve adapting any item to become part of the child's play experience.

For some children, it may mean playing in a warm bath, using bubbles, low lights and soft music; for others, it may mean playing in mud and sand, screaming and making loud noises.

It does not have to cost anything and can be very simple. This book encourages you to think imaginatively and consider how sensory play can be incorporated into almost any activity using everyday items.

Why is it important?

We have recognised that we make sense of the world around us by using our senses. By encouraging enhanced use of our senses we can help stimulate and support children to be more receptive and aware of their world. It can help children interpret the world around them and teach them how to respond appropriately.

Children benefit from increased physical interaction, communication and imagination, a greater physical awareness and may learn to have a greater awareness of danger. Sensory play can also enhance social, emotional and cognitive development. It is non-threatening, especially for children who have low self-esteem or who are unable to participate in other kinds of play.

Some children can use sensory play to help take away aggression or to feel calmer and more secure in a low sensory arousal atmosphere. Others specifically need the stimulation that can come from sensory play.

We have spoken about taking a child-centred approach looking at the sensory activities from their point of view. We need to engage with the child and be a part of their experience, but not take over the play opportunity. Our role is to enable play and support the child to participate fully.

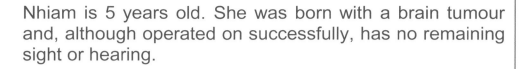

Nhiam is 5 years old. She was born with a brain tumour and, although operated on successfully, has no remaining sight or hearing.

To Nhiam, touch is how she makes sense of the world. Her favourite activity is to sit on top of a stereo speaker and 'feel' the music through the vibrations on her bottom!

She loves to play her dad's guitar; she dances and sings to the beat and particularly enjoys 1960s' music!

If you are working or living with a child or young person who cannot intellectualise and understand the purpose of a toy or activity or complete a task, sensory play is essential, giving the child opportunity to participate. A great benefit of sensory play is that there does not have to be a finished product; play exists for the sake of play.

Consider a child who is unable to read a recipe and make a cake. For him, the experience of running his hands through flour and feeling how the mixture changes when you add water is far more enjoyable than struggling to reach an end goal.

Many children have low self-esteem and confidence when they do not feel they can achieve an end result. With sensory play, the experience is the product of play and the child does not have to feel pressured to succeed.

Some children may hate sensory play, particularly messy play, getting dirty, muddy, wet or touching substances they find uncomfortable. Consider the barriers and think about how these may be overcome.

Ben developed an aversion to the sensation of touching water. The situation became difficult when his parents could not get him to bath or wash. He drank through a straw but would not allow the drink to touch his lips.

Through sensory play, he became accustomed to touching bubbles and eventually was happy to take a bubble bath provided that he could not see the water beneath the layer of bubbles. Although this was not a complete solution, it was certainly a step in the right direction.

14

Each child or young person will respond to sensory play differently, which is why is it essential to take a person-centred approach when offering sensory experiences.

Consider what you need to know about the child or young person before you start to introduce sensory play. Never force a child into an experience they are withdrawing from; instead, offer a lead by undertaking the activity yourself and encourage the child to experiment at their own level.

How do we know that a child is enjoying the activity?
All children are able to communicate in some way, even though they may not use speech to express their feelings. Behaviour is form of communication so, as you introduce new experiences, look for the types of behaviour that are being exhibited. These will tell you if you the child likes or dislikes the experience.

Make a note of activities that the child has or has not enjoyed. Try to expand the activities you know the child has enjoyed by adding new sensations. We need to watch children's behaviour, and recognise the difference between enjoyment, fear or discomfort.

Remember that fear or dislike may be a barrier to participation. However, don't let the behaviour stop you thinking about the activity from the child's perspective and recognise what you may need to put into place to reduce the barriers.

At an Early Years setting, the staff introduced the children to messy play by offering an activity using water and cornflour. The children enjoyed putting their hands into the bowl and mixing the ingredients, feeling the sensations on their hands and between their fingers.

Sam, who happened to have autism, looked on. He was interested in the activity, but pulled away as soon as a worker encouraged him to get involved. He did not like getting his hands dirty!

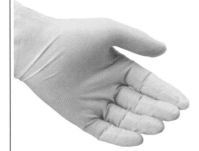 The staff member offered Sam a pair of small examination gloves. Once he was wearing them he was happy to put his hands into the mixture. He could 'feel' the same sensations but did not get his hands dirty. The barrier to participation had been broken down.

The staff at Sam's setting could have decided that, as he did not like the activity, they would not offer that opportunity again. However, with a little thought and understanding, barriers were broken down and he was able to participate. This in turn led to his participation in many other sensory play activities.

Some children will laugh and giggle, others will have different pitches of scream or will grind their teeth and some may run away or hide. Others may use a form of augmented communication such as symbol cards or photographs.

If you are working with a child or young person and are not sure how to recognise emotions then ask the parent or guardian for help, and keep observing. If you are working with children who have little verbal communication you will need to identify the meaning behind the behaviour.

Parents want to know what their child has done during the day. Many children will benefit from keeping a diary of activities. Taking photographs with permission is a great way to record the child's response to sensory stimuli and can help the parent to undertake similar play at home.

We have included some quick and easy 5 minute sensory play activity idea sheets at the back of this book, ideal to do at home.

If the child has difficulty in communicating their emotions, help them to choose an appropriate emotion face to illustrate the level of their enjoyment. Add these to the diary in order to pass on information to other adults to help them plan appropriate sensory plan activities in the future.

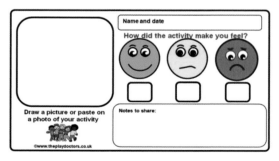   

We have included a simple activity diary template in the photocopy pages. Use this or make your own with the children.

Using sensory play to reduce stress and help children calm down

Sensory play can also be used to support a child to calm down if they are upset. Using water, massage and gentle touch, coloured lights and soft music may be appropriate for some; others will calm down when they are in a low arousal area. Be aware of individual calming techniques.

If you feel a child is getting to the stage of sensory overload, consider using a quiet area for a few minutes. It does not have to be a specifically built dark or white room. If a child is stressed, a short time out in a pop-up tent or a den can work well.

The theory of colour

For many years, people have recognised how humans can be affected by different colours. The theory is used in the types of packaging that is used for food through to the colour with which strip cells in prisons are decorated. Take a quick look at the colour box illustrated. What colours would you choose to represent anger, fear, anxiety, fun or excitement?

Take another look, this time considering what colours you feel are calming. It is important to recognise how important colour is in a child's life. If the child(ren) you are working with is able to tell you, ask them the same questions. You may be surprised; they may choose a different colour from your own.

The theory of colour tells us that bright red is a very emotionally intense colour. It stands out from other colours and has a high visibility, which is why it is used in traffic lights, stop signs and fire engines. It is also seen as an 'aggressive' colour and has the longest wavelength on the colour spectrum. Yellow is seen as a 'happy' colour associated with increased brain activity and energy. It is also an attention grabber; hence, yellow safety clothing and yellow cabs in the USA. Orange combines the energy of red and the happiness of yellow.

Green is the colour of nature, promoting harmony and peace, and blue is considered beneficial to the mind; it slows human metabolism and produces a calming effect. Pale lilac is also seen as a calming colour, and the majority of pre-adolescent children prefer purple and lilac to any other colour. Lilac and blue are also easy on the eye. Primary colours are not calming.

Consider your own quiet areas. Are you using low arousal colours or stimulating colours? Think about how you can introduce pale greens, blues and lilacs.

The therapeutic use of weight

The use of weight and pressure is well recognised as a calming method to help both children and adults. It is used with individuals who have symptoms of stress, depression and anxiety. It can also be used for children who have difficulty with muscle control.

Weight has proven beneficial to support anxiety in children who are on the autism spectrum, who have ADHD, dyspraxia and many other conditions. Be aware of personal preference; this technique is **not** appropriate for all children. If concerned then take advice from a health professional before using weight.

There are many ways to introduce weight through items such as large weighted blankets, small lap blankets, weighted waistcoats, wrist and ankle weights and even weighted cuddly toys. These are available from specialist retailers but tend to be expensive. On occasion, they may be supplied by a medical health professional such as an OT.

Phoebe happens to have autism. She often gets too loud, noisy and aggressive towards others. She constantly runs and climbs. She pulls off her clothes if they are loose; she prefers items that are tight or too small. She also has erratic sleep patterns. Her parents noticed that she slept better when she was rolled up tight in a sleeping bag with extra blankets.

When attending a local club the play workers introduced a series of tactile mats during a sensory play session, including a large, heavy rubber floor mat. Phoebe climbed beneath the mat and lay still. The staff recognised that she calmed down when under the weight of the mat. They purchased a wheat-filled neck wrap, which she enjoyed having placed over her shoulders.

At home, Mum made a simple weighted blanket. Phoebe's sleeping patterns improved and she calmed down at the end of the day by sitting beneath the blanket while watching television. Mum also made a simple fabric weighted snake that Phoebe enjoyed placing over her shoulders.

What else do we need to know?

Apart from understanding the child's individual responses to sensory stimuli it is also important to recognise anything that may affect your sensory play planning. Does the child have any particular allergies you need to be aware of? Is there any cultural reason that you should not touch the child?

Be aware of any underlying impairments the child may have that will affect their response to sensory play, for example, a child who has a visual impairment may not enjoy playing with sight activities that use reflections. A child who has autism may not enjoy making musical instruments if they have a sensitivity to sound.

Always prepare the child for the activity. Some children may like to see pictures of what they are about to do, or to be introduced to the activity slowly, especially if it is a new concept for them.

If the child reacts strongly to sensory overload, do you know what methods are already used to help them calm down?

Sylvie seemed to be enjoying the planned sensory play session. She was sitting with a play worker, happily using a wooden spoon and banging it on a saucepan. All of a sudden, she looked up; other children were also making loud noises. Sylvie stood up, put her hands over her ears and started to spin in a circle…

The play worker had no idea that Sylvie would respond in such a manner when she initially seemed to be enjoying the experience. The activity was acceptable when she could concentrate on her own actions. However, at a critical point the noise level in the room became too much and she could not cope.

A staff member who had previously worked with Sylvie, recognised the fact that she had sensory overload and needed some support to help cut down the overwhelming sensation of audio input.

She reached out and passed Sylvie a pair of ear defenders.

Once Sylvie put them on she calmed down and was happy to participate in a different activity.

19

If you are aware of a child's particular sensitivity, pass that information on to others, especially if you know what may help calm a child down. Be aware of the individual children and their personal preferences, needs and requirements.

A child who has difficulty holding and controlling a paintbrush may instead enjoy using finger paints. The child may find this easier to master, and the use of tactile paint gives them an opportunity to 'feel' the activity in addition to seeing the result.

Children who may not have the dexterity to finger paint may enjoy the feeling of 'being painted' using a wide soft brush on their arms or legs.

Some children may have multiple needs and lack the ability to control their own play. Instead, they may love to feel the wind on their face, a ribbon run over their skin or enjoy the sensation of their wheelchair being pushed over cobblestones.

Always consider the activity from the child's perspective and recognise how they communicate their enjoyment or anxiety.

Communication passports are particularly useful for sharing information. They are normally simple sheets indicating likes/dislikes, communication methods, sensitivities and other useful information.

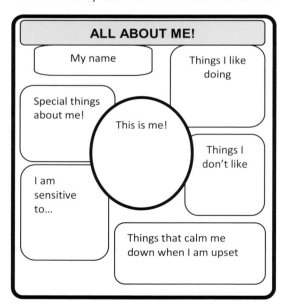

Some children may have difficulty in imagining what they want to make from a range of scrap paper or how to engage in sensory play. It is good to have suggestions available or even theme the ideas around their favourite characters in a story. Examples include the magic of Harry Potter, Shrek's swamp or using Thomas the Tank Engine as the basis for creative play. Talk to the children and encourage them to tell you about their interests. Work within those parameters to begin with.

photocopy

We have included two communication passports* templates in the photocopy resource pages. Use these or develop your own.

*Further information on the use of communication passports can be found in 'It's not all about talking', a further practical resource book written by Wendy Usher and published by The Play Doctors IBSN9780956669063

20

Sensory Play Activities

This section provides ideas for many diverse sensory play activities. Use the ideas pages as a starting point. Adapt any activity so that it is appropriate for the child(ren) you are playing with.

Key to symbols:

  When you see this sign, the activity is appropriate to all ages, including babies. Be aware that for some children their developmental stage is younger than their chronological age.

When you see these signs, the activities are suitable for Early Years (EY ages 2-4) and Primary Plus (P+ ages 5 and upwards). Activities may be adapted for older children. Look out for extension activity ideas.

The picture symbols relate to the primary sense(s) used within the activity.

Touch   Sight   Hearing   Taste   Smell   Balance   Body Awareness

 Resources available to freely photocopy.

photocopy

We advise you to check that any paints or colourants used in these ideas will not stain.

22

Chapter Two
Creating sensory play:
Playing with touch

All

**Creating a sensory floor space
Equipment**
bathmat/doormat/ cushions/ newspaper/ fleece/piece of carpet/bamboo mat/bubble wrap/furry rug

Whatever is available to use in your home or setting.

Sensory idea
Try putting out the different tactile surfaces in a tent or in a cardboard box to create a den. Expand the idea for sensory stimulation by hanging ribbons or strips of fabric from the ceiling of the den.

Experiment by turning the lights off in the room. See if the children can identify the various surfaces.

Touch is one of the key senses we use to explore and experiment with the world around us. It varies from a physical touch, for example, the warm feeling of being wrapped in a blanket, through to the light sensation of feeling the breeze on our face or the wind in our hair.

This chapter provides lots of ideas to be creative in activities. Always consider how you can extend the activities or adapt them according to the children you are working with.

Creating a sensory touch environment
Sensory floor space
Take a look around and have a think about what is available to you to create a tactile sensory floor space full of different textures.

Use whatever is to hand, and allow the children to freely explore. They may wish to roll, crawl, slide or walk on the various surfaces. Some children may just like to lie still on a particular tactile surface.

23

Sensory outdoor pathway

Equipment
trays of sand/water/
rice/bubble wrap or
anything you have to
hand.

Sensory idea
Try putting different
materials in trays filled
with water and
bubbles. The children
are not going to see
what kind of textures
they will be stepping
on and the activity
becomes more
exciting.

Sensory outdoor pathway

When playing outside, experiment by providing the children with a different surface play path using trays of sand, water, earth, rice, bubble wrap or any other materials you have available suitable for outside use. Allow children to walk barefooted to feel the textures.

For wheelchair users, try gluing pebbles on to thick card and allow the child to experience the sensation of bumps while the chair is pushed over the stones.

Sensory wall panels

Consider how you can expand this idea and create a sensory wall panel. Areas of tactile wall surfaces can be used to help children follow a passage between two rooms using touch.

Consider what you can use that will be durable. Plastic grass matting can be purchased in different colours and cut into strips to be fixed to a wall.

Small wooden or plastic garden trellis can be wall mounted to create a durable panel. Experiment by threading through different textured materials.

The example on the left was made by children using anything they had to hand threaded through plastic netting. They used fine yellow net cut from a bath scrub. In this, they encased corks and pine cones and a plastic triangle that they had found. They also used some wooden curtain rings, shiny fabric, wool and tinsel. During the making of this, we talked about what they could see, feel or hear.

Bath scrubs are made from a long netting tube. Look for the string that ties the scrub together and snip through. Separate out the netting tube, which can be used for many sensory play ideas.

Sensory touch books
Equipment
card for the book pages/
glue and double-sided
tape/scissors/pens
(or print pages from a
computer)/various
representational
materials/ring binder*

*The pages can be
stored in a ring binder,
which allows extra pages
to be added at a later
date. We used a small
A5 ring binder.

**We have suggested
representational
materials in relation to
this activity, but
encourage children to
find their own!**

**Remember the
illustrations are
examples only. Allow
the child(ren) to
participate in making
their own book.**

**Our book
about being
outside**
by Nyasha & Rutendo

Sensory touch book

It is far more exciting for children to be involved in the creation of a touch book, rather than just buying one. When making the book, consider the child's own particular interests, and incorporate these ideas. The book does not have to follow a story; it can just have simple 'touch' pages with things that are soft, hard, bumpy, slippery, etc.

In the example provided, Nyasha and Rutendo decided that they liked playing outside at Grandma's house. They listed the things they liked about being outside:

- The sun
- The rain
- Watering the plants
- Finding daisies
- Planting seeds
- Playing in the sand
- Feeding the fish in the pond

Depending on the individual child, the book can be very simple or more complicated.

We have included some 'extension ideas' to provide some interactive activities. Work with the child(ren) and support them to have choice and control in their decision making. Your role is to act as an enabler, enhancing their play choices rather than taking over, although help may be needed when making the book.

Take the children outside for a walk. Talk to them about what they can see, hear, smell and touch. Look for further materials within the home or your setting. It does not need to be complicated; small bits and pieces make fabulous items to put in a sensory touch book.

25

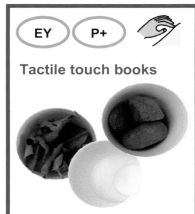

EY **P+**

Tactile touch books

When we play outside we see the sky.

Sunshine page
Equipment
blue paper/pipe cleaners/mirror card disk (or use shiny paper)

Sometimes it rains but we still go outside.

Rain page
Equipment
photograph/shiny holographic paper

Write short sentences to create a story. Consider adding in photographs. Remember, the ideas are for you to work with and to adapt as you prefer. Explore the book gently with eyes closed. What can the child feel? Can they guess what is on the pages?

If the child does not want to make a sensory touch book, or does not have the dexterity or cognitive ability to do so, encourage them to collect things together and put them in a sensory touch bag, touch box, or even in plastic cups.

Sunshine page Use a piece of shiny paper or mirror card to make a sunshine. The rays of the sunshine are made from pipe cleaners. Ask the child to feel the surfaces. Are they soft or hard, warm or cold?

Extension activity Take this page outside. Ask the child if they can see the sky and the sunshine reflected in the shiny paper or mirror card. Play with reflections. What else can the child see outside? What can they hear?

Rain page Cut out simple raindrop shapes from holographic or shiny paper and do the same for the puddle and stick them on to the page. Feel the surface. Does it feel slippery like water?

Extension activity Experiment by making puddles on different surfaces. Pour water on to sand, mud, the pavement, grass and other surfaces. See if the water creates a puddle or is absorbed.

If indoors, try making mini puddles in bowls by pouring water on to different materials such as modelling clay, a sponge or cornflour.

Talk to the children about how the surfaces feel using descriptive language such as 'squelchy', 'slippery', 'oozy', 'sticky' or 'slimy'. Ask them what else they can think of that these words describe. Use their ideas, find appropriate resources and try touching their suggestions.

We like finding daisies

Daisy page
Equipment
photograph/a piece of ribbon/felt and yellow sticker dots

It is fun watering the plants

Watering plants
Equipment
photograph/shiny buttons/straws/tissue paper

Sometimes we plant seeds

Planting seeds
Equipment:
photograph/various seeds

Daisy page Use fabric or felt to cut out some daisy shapes. Stick these to the page. We have also added a piece of flower ribbon that was in the setting.

Extension activity Try adding a little perfume to the felt pieces. The scent will be absorbed into the felt and will remain for some time. Top up as necessary.

Watering plants page Here we have represented drops of water by using shiny buttons. Flowers are represented by tissue paper and straws are used for stems.

Extension activity Find lots of buttons, counters, pasta or rice. Put them into a container and pour them gently on to a plastic tray so that they sound like water droplets falling. Experiment with different materials and pour them on to different surfaces such as a tin tray.

Planting seeds page Collect seeds in the autumn months; save them in paper bags for future use. Seeds are also readily available from garden centres and supermarkets.

Extension activity Purchase a selection of seasonal seeded fruit such as apples, oranges or strawberries. Ask the children to find the seeds. Some are on the outside of fruits and others on the inside.

Use the fruit to make some fruit kebabs, and eat! Sort the fruit into piles based on texture, colour, smell and types. Does the fruit smell the same before and after it is cut?

Talk to the children about the size and shapes of different seeds. Look up pictures to see what the plants look like that the seeds have come from.

Get the children to lay seeds out on a surface or tray. Sort them into groups or use them to make faces or pictures.

We play in the sand,
it is soft between our toes
and rough when we rub
it on our skin.

**Playing in sand
equipment**
sandpaper/soft fabric/
photograph

We like feeding the fish

**Feeding the fish
Equipment**
Shiny fabric/bubble wrap/
small coins

It's fun outside!

Playing in sand page Chat to the children about how sand feels. Sometimes, it can be rough on your skin or feels very soft when you walk on it and it gets in-between your toes.

Use the sandpaper to represent rough sand and soft fabric to represent soft sand. Velvet or felt works well.

Extension activity Try piling sand up high in the sandpit or in a tray. Experiment by balancing on one leg, hopping, walking and jumping. If you are doing this activity in a tray, try balancing objects on top of the pile of sand. Ask if it easier to walk in sand or on the pavement. Try burying things in the sand and asking the child to find you something hard, something soft, something round, something long or short.

Feeding the fish Talk about the fish. What colour are they? Can the children see bubbles in the water? We used shiny glitter fabric for the fish (this was from a glittery party dress purchased from a charity shop). Bubble wrap was used to create tactile water and small coins were used to represent bubbles.

Extension activities Put water in a glass bowl and add a little hypo-allergenic washing-up liquid (always check for sensitivity). Optional: add scent and food colouring to the water.

Create some small fish by cutting them out of silver foil, paper or plastic. For more exciting fish, try cutting them from pieces of raw carrot. These can then be eaten later! Put them in the bowl to see if they sink or float. Use a straw to gently blow the fish around the surface of the water. Put the straw into the water and blow. If you are using a glass bowl, the children can see the bubbles form under the water and float up.

Talk about the image in the book. Feel the materials used. Try adding a few coins to the water. Ask the children to use their hands to 'dive' and retrieve the coins.

28

Growing a daisy
Equipment
card to cut out daisy
head/backing card/lollypop
stick or something similar
for stem/stiff fabric to
represent earth

Spinning daisy
Equipment
card to cut out daisy
head/backing card/split pin/
plastic straw

Further extension activities to make the tactile sensory touch book interactive

Growing a daisy

Draw and cut out a simple daisy head. Colour as desired and glue to a small stick to act as the stem. Lollipop sticks work well. Choose a piece of card or fabric to make the earth and cut slightly wider than the head of the daisy. Place a strip of glue on each side edge of the earth fabric (or card). Glue on to the backing card, arching it up slightly, leaving sufficient room to 'post' the daisy between the backing card and the earth.

The daisy can be 'grown' by pushing the stick upwards, or waved from side to side in the wind by swinging the stick from left to right and back again.

Ideas Draw or print pictures of small bugs, flies, worms or caterpillars. Attach them to small sticks and post these sticks behind the earth fabric or card as you did with the daisy. These creatures will be hidden until they pop up by sliding the stick up gently.

Take children outside to feel the earth with their hands. Ask if it hard, soft, warm or cold. Allow the children to dig in the mud with their hands and make mud pies! Try digging for worms, and carefully get the children to hold them in their hands. Always put worms back on to soft earth after playing.

Spinning daisy Try making a spinning daisy. Use the same daisy template you made earlier. Cut out the daisies and attach to the backing card by using a split pin. This works better if you add a small washer between the back of the split pin and the backing sheet. We have used a small piece of plastic straw but you can also use a button or a washer.

Fold over one side of each petal, allowing the daisy to catch the wind. This can be 'blown' around (similar to a windmill) or pushed around using a finger or pencil.

Simple tactile page
Equipment
samples of previous
materials used

Be aware that some children may not be able to intellectualise the concepts within the ideas suggested. For these children, you may wish to just create single pages of one texture or type of material.

Touch board
Equipment
card/glue/scissors/various
sensory materials that you
have to hand

Simple tactile page

Finally in this section, we have suggested creating a simple page utilising the materials used previously. Simply glue samples of the materials on to a backing sheet and ask the child what the materials feel like, look like and what they remind the child of in the book. Search through the book to find the matching materials.

Idea   Attach a range of materials from the sensory touch book on to card. Use the same materials and place them on a tray. Cover the tray with a cloth. The child reaches under the cloth and feels an object or piece of material. He then looks at the card and guesses which material he has touched.

Creating sensory surfaces

Touch boards (All)

Start with a piece of heavy cardboard (such as the side of a cardboard box). Look for items that you have available and cover the board with different surfaces to feel. We have included: bubble wrap; fur fabric; felt; glitter; split pins; plastic; foam; sticks; metal; and ribbon.

On the board illustrated we have used plastic document binders to edge the board on three sides and foam pipe insulation on the fourth side.

Idea Create an activity touch board where things move or make noises. The board illustrated uses a bell bracelet (borrowed from the noise making box) an old belt cut from a shoulder bag and a piece of thin skipping rope.

> Ben is 6 years old. He happens to be on the autism spectrum and loves this simple board. He spends hours running his hands over the bells, undoes and does up the belt and makes bows with the skipping rope.
>
> This very simple activity is more popular than expensive equipment and toys.

Metallic touch board Equipment
soft drinks can/sharp scissors/pad of paper/ball point pen/tape to seal edges of aluminium sheet

Metallic touch board

As an extension to this theme we have created a sensory touch surface made from the inside of a soft drink can. Children will need help and supervision with this activity. Always use a heavy tape to seal sharp edges.

Wash the can out and carefully split it open with a pair of sharp scissors, cutting off the top and the base. Use thin aluminium cans as they are easier to cut. Trim sharp edges off the remaining aluminium sheet. Stick thick tape such as a double layer of masking tape over sharp edges.

Place the panel you have cut out on to a thick pad of paper, shiny side down. Draw or write on to the printed side of the aluminium using a ball point pen. Use more pressure than normal. This will create a raised impression on the reverse side. Check that the indentation has worked. If not, try again adding a little more pressure.

Experiment with different types of ball point pens. Those with fine writing nibs are better for this activity. Be careful that you do not puncture the aluminium.

Use the panel to create a tactile, 'feely' surface. In the example above we simply created a series of shapes. We enhanced this panel by including buttons, eyelets and brads that were in the craft box.

Try writing simple words on the aluminium, then use it as a stamp with an ink pad. Ask the children to experiment. How does the printed image look? Work with the children to recognise that the writing needs to be written in reverse in order to print out correctly. Discuss this with the children and explore the activity by using mirrors and reflection. Try using different things to imprint into the aluminium such as the end or the nib of a pencil. Feel the metal. It should feel cool.

31

Creating sensory touch games

Sensory twister game

Select and glue a range of tactile items to a piece of card or fabric that is laid out on the floor. Use pieces of the same materials and glue on to the sides of a small square box to create a sensory dice. One child is responsible for throwing the dice. In turn, the other children place either a hand or foot on to the mat as indicated by the surface shown on the dice.

Idea Think about how you can adapt this activity. Try hiding different materials around the setting and throwing the dice. The child needs to seek out the appropriate item or material and bring it back to you.

Tic-Tac-Toe (0s & Xs)

You do not need paper and pencils to play this game. Provided a grid is laid out, it is possible to use anything.

Here we have illustrated the game using materials that are hard or soft. Instead of 0s and Xs the players are using buttons and felt disks with straws laid out for the grid.

Tic-Tac-Toe using water

Try a different game using cardboard and a bowl of water. Instead of using a pen have a game using water drawn on by using a finger. After the water has evaporated you are ready to start again. Try adding a little scent to the water to create a new sensory experience.

Idea Take the idea of using water to create an image a little further by painting with water on to paving stones on a hot day and watching them dry. Experiment by making water footprints and handprints.

Make a pinprick in a balloon and fill the balloon with water. Squeeze the balloon gently and draw with the expelled water on to paving stones. Try laying down an object and spraying over it so that the outline is left on the paving stone.

P+

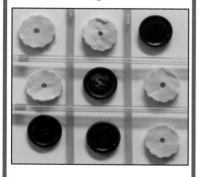

Sensory twister game
Equipment
large piece of card/small square cardboard box/glue or double-sided tape/ various materials that are tactile such as straws, wood, fabric, bubble wrap, felt, fur, corrugated card

Tic-Tac-Toe
Equipment
backing card/buttons/felt shapes/straws

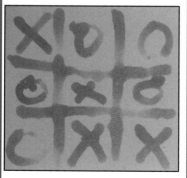

Tic-Tac-Toe water game
Equipment
backing card
water
finger! **EY** **P+**

Home-made finger paints Equipment
2 large tablespoons of sugar
½ cup of cornflour
2 cups of cold water
¼ cup of washing-up liquid (clear liquid is best or it will 'tint' your mixture)/food colouring or powder paints/saucepan for cooking/ container for storage

Frozen ice boats Equipment
water
paint or food colouring/ice cube tray or other container/straws or sticks/paper for sails/scent (if wanted)/freezer

Home-made finger paints

Gather the ingredients listed. Mix the sugar and corn flour together in a small saucepan. Slowly add the water, stirring all the time. Once the contents are mixed together, cook over a low heat and keep stirring. The mixture will start to thicken and then 'gel'. Keep stirring until the mixture is smooth and almost clear.

Let the mixture cool down. Once cool, add the washing-up liquid and food colouring or powder paints. Keep stirring until the mixture is smooth and has absorbed the entire colour. The mixture can be kept in the fridge for up to three days. Powder paints will create stronger colours.

Idea Try adding a few drops of different scents to the various colours. Ask the children if they can identify the colour by the scent alone. Create different textures by adding fine sand or rice.

Make a bowlful of finger paint. Hide various objects in the bowl and allow the children to place their whole hand into the mixture and guess what items they can feel.

Spread the mixture on to a plastic or metal tray. Ask the children to draw into the mixture by using their finger. When they want a new drawing re-spread the mixture back over the tray and start again. Try doing the same thing on bubble wrap and allow the children to 'feel' the bubbles through the paint.

Floating ice boats

Fill an ice cube tray with water, add colouring if desired. Place short pieces of straw in each section to make a mast. Cut pieces of paper to make sails, thread over the straw once the cube is frozen. Play with these in a bowl of warm water. Children can feel both warm and cold.

Listen for the cubes 'clinking' against each other, and cracking with the warmth of the water. Watch the ice cubes melt and discharge their colour into the water.

33

**Ice cube paints
Equipment**
water/paint/ice cube tray or
other container/straws or
sticks/freezer

**Ice marbles
Equipment**
Water/balloons/freezer

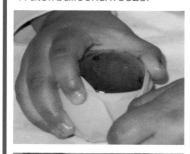

Experiment by freezing water in different containers and bowls. Small cake moulds are easy to use to create shapes or characters, or make your own moulds from soft clay. Carefully place a straw in each mould before freezing to act as a mast.

Once frozen, cut a piece of paper into a square shape. Cut two simple slots in the paper and thread it over the straw to create a sail. Place in water and blow on the sails to race the ice boats.

Try adding scent to the water prior to freezing. Ask the children to tell you what they can smell. The activity is short-lived as the ice cubes quickly melt, but the experience for the children is worth the effort.

If the children are in agreement, run an ice cube up and down their arms or legs to create a different sensory experience.

Ice cube paints

Mix some powder paint in water (or use a water-based paint), pour into ice cube trays and freeze to create ice cube paints. If the children do not like the sensation of holding a frozen cube of paint, add a small lolly stick to each cube before freezing to provide a handle for the child to hold.

Ice marbles

Fill some balloons with different coloured water. This is easier to do if you stretch the neck of the balloon around a cone (see image). Experiment by pushing small plastic figurines into the balloon to encapsulate them in ice! Freeze the balloons. Once they are frozen, cut the rubber balloon away from the ice. Play with them in warm water so that the children's hands do not get too cold, and watch the figures emerge.

We made an ice age mammoth by freezing a small plastic elephant in our balloon.

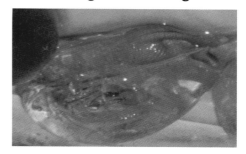

Frozen hands
Equipment
rubber or latex glove/water/colourant (optional)/freezer

Feely bags
Equipment
bag or pillowcase/balloons or gloves/various tactile fillings

EY   P+

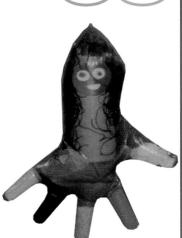

Feely Bob
Equipment
plastic or latex glove/whatever materials you have to hand.
Feely Bob was made by students attending Sensory Play Training led by The Play Doctors

Creating a frozen hand

Fill a latex glove with water, wrap an elastic band around the wrist and place it in the freezer.

Once frozen, let the children feel the 'frozen hand'. Fill another glove with warm water and ask the children to compare hot and cold. Peel the glove off the frozen water and create hand-shaped ice cubes. This is easier to do if you first dip the frozen hand into warm water for a few seconds.

Try adding a little food colouring or glitter to the water before putting it in the glove for added effect.

Unusual feely bags

Experiment with other substances in balloons or gloves such as cornflour and water, rice, sand (wet and dry), flour, jelly or even wallpaper paste! Try placing the balloons or gloves in a pillowcase, box or drawstring bag. Get the children to feel the objects and talk about what they feel. If you make sets of two with the same fillings, children can play 'feely pairs'.

What other ideas do you have for using balloon and examination gloves in play?

Sensory scrap Feely Bob

We have spoken about using materials that are readily available around you. In this illustration, 'Feely Bob' was created from a plastic glove and anything that was to hand, including a cardboard tube, black wool, rice, lentils, jelly (in one of the fingers!), soft fabric and cotton wool.

It really does not matter what goes inside the glove; the aim is to create as many textures and visual stimuli as you can. Get the children to make this with you or make one for themselves.

Ask the children to describe the sensations hard, soft or squishy, and decide what he has been made out of. This activity is designed to be made for a single play session. There is virtually no cost involved and the fun is to remake another to replace the activity.

Gloop
Equipment
1 cup of cornflour/water to mix/bowl

Directions
Knead ingredients together until they form a silly putty ball. This will take a few minutes. Continue until the wetness goes away.
If it is wet and the mixture is not bonding, add more cornflour. If it is dry, add more glue.

Store in an airtight container. It will keep happily in the fridge for a few days.

Silly putty
Equipment
1 cup of white glue
2 cups of cornflour

Interesting facts
Gloop is known scientifically as a 'non-Newtonian' substance; neither liquid nor solid but both. By stirring it quickly it behaves more like a solid, or by leaving it alone it reverts to being a liquid.

Creating messy play opportunities

Even very young children will benefit from participating in messy play. With a little support, all children are able to take part. Be aware of any sensitivity and respond accordingly. This section provides a range of ideas allowing the children freedom to explore the senses through different substances.

The world of messy play is limitless. Think of how you can expand any of these activities and build on the ideas provided. If the child does not want to touch messy materials, encourage them to feel through a plastic bag. Encourage the children to explore messy play for themselves.

Making gloop

Simply mix cornflour and water together. Get the children to mix it with their fingers, stirring until the mixture becomes glutinous and thick. Experiment with the quantities of cornflour to water as different ratios will provide different densities.

If the mixture is left alone, the cornflour will fall to the bottom of the mixture. Allow the children to put their hands into the bowl and 'dig' for gloop. Once this is lifted from the water it becomes thick strands of glutinous gel, as illustrated. Add colourant as desired.

If you have access to a large tray such as a sand or water tray, try making a large batch of the mixture and allow the children to step into it barefoot. If the children jump up and down, the cornflour will remain solid. If they move slowly, the mixture it will become sticky and slimy. Children love this activity; the mixture will easily wash off their skin. Wait for any splashes to dry before brushing off clothing. Why not try it in the bath?

Silly putty

To create a denser gloop, replace the water with white glue. This allows the mixture to become more like modelling clay: it can be broken and re-moulded. Use a little food colouring or powder paints to create a range of colours. Be aware of staining, and carefully read the instructions on the colouring agent before use.

36

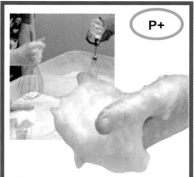

Soap slime
Equipment
pure soap flakes (Lux or similar)/water/food colouring/bowl/whisk

Ideas
Start off by making a soap solution for jelly soap and leave it a few hours to set. Allow the children to play with it by making hand imprints, breaking it up and running it through their fingers.

Add a little more water and start to whisk the solution. The 'jelly' will dissolve and turn into bubbles to create soapy slime.

Once the solution is whisked, divide between several bowls. Add a few drops of pre-mixed poster paint (a very small amount) and drag the paintbrush through the surface of the solution. The paint will spread and create wonderful swirl patterns. Try adding colours together.

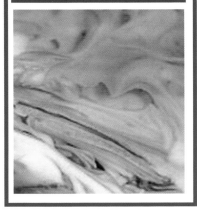

Making soapy slime
Prior to undertaking this activity, be aware of soap sensitivity or any allergies. This activity is messy and can leave the floor quite slippery. It is best done outside on a nice sunny day.

To make soapy slime, mix 1 cup of pure soap flakes (Lux flakes or other brand), 3 cups of warm water and a few drops of food colouring (if desired) in a large bowl. Beat the mixture using a hand whisk or electric whisk. The mixture will treble in size, so make sure you use a large bowl. The faster you beat, the smaller the bubbles and the more dense the mixture.

Sensory idea
Make two batches of soap slime using primary colours. Leave the children to experiment while playing, and see if they can change the colour of the slime by adding the two colours together, i.e. red + yellow = orange.

Extension activity: creating jelly-like soap P+
The ingredients remain the same as above. To make a jelly substance, poor boiling or very hot water on to the soap flakes. Stir gently until all the soap flakes are completely dissolved. Do not whip. Leave the substance for a few hours to set; the longer you leave it the thicker it will become.

Enhancing play  EY   P+
Think about what is available to you to enhance the play experience for the child. Hide objects in the soap for the children to find. Ask the children to take handfuls of slime and run it across different textured surfaces such as bubble wrap, silver foil or sandpaper. If you are brave, place a large plastic sheet on the ground and allow the children to slide about in the slime. It's messy, but they will certainly remember the experience!

37

Wobbly jelly soap

P+

Equipment
2 packets of gelatine/½ cup of water/½ cup of liquid soap such as shampoo or body wash/scent as desired/small objects to encapsulate such as flowers or leaves

Wobbly jelly soap

Dissolve 2 packs of gelatine in a ½ cup of boiling water and mix thoroughly. Add a ½ cup of liquid soap and whatever scent you choose unless the liquid soap is already fragranced. Sweet scent such as cherry works well. Pour the mixture into inexpensive plastic jelly moulds or use ice cube trays or other containers. Let the mixture set. Experiment by adding an unexpected scent, for example, strawberry for yellow soap or lemon for red soap.

You have now created mini soap bars that can be played with in warm water. The soap becomes very slippery and is difficult to hold.

Try placing small objects such as flowers or leaves into the ice cube tray prior to pouring in the soap jelly. The jelly will encase the object, which will be 'found' once the soap has dissolved. Try layering different colours to create rainbow soaps.

Sensory idea

Cook some spaghetti and let it cool. Add it to the soap so that the children can explore and find 'worms'! Pour food colouring into the water prior to cooking the spaghetti; it will absorb the colour and create wonderful coloured worms. Ask the children for their own ideas.

Creating soap crayons

This is an opportunity to use up all the old bits of soap. Grate them all into a large bowl using a fine food grater. Divide the mixture into several bowls and add a few drops of warm water and natural food colouring to each bowl. Mix each bowl until the ingredients have combined. Pick up the mixture and play with it to create soap dough. Once the dough is smooth, roll sausage shapes for soap crayons or whatever shape you wish. Once completed, put in the freezer for 10 minutes (helps the soap bind together) before putting in a warm place until dry (can take up to 2 days).

(All)

Massage Equipment
warm water/flour/body lotion (hypoallergenic)/baby oil/soft sand/brushes/ sponges/baby wipes/ natural sponges

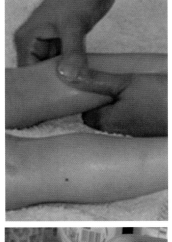

Body touch and massage

So far in this section the messy play activities have all involved using hands. It is important to remember that the sensation of touch can happen all over the body. Some children may prefer to be touched on their arms, legs or even their feet.

We regularly hear of face painting, but don't always extend the idea to other parts of the body. Experiment with a range of different substances to paint or massage on to the body, and ask the children how it feels. Use thin and wide brushes, sponges, fingers and hands to paint with.

Ideas using different textures

Try creating a mixture of warm water and flour. Use a wide brush and paint the mixture across the children's arms and legs. Allow to dry. The thin crust will crack on touch or movement. Allow the children to pick the dried flour and water mixture off their skin. If they do not like the sensation, wash off with warm water.

Try massaging skin using body lotion. For children who prefer a different type of touch, experiment by using soft sand mixed into the body lotion. Ensure the sand is not abrasive on the skin.

Experiment by squirting water on to skin using an old, clean washing-up bottle. Use warm and cold water to do this. Children who prefer a firm touch will benefit from a direct stream of water, holding the bottle near to the body. Children who prefer a gentle touch will value the feeling of water being dripped on to their body.

Experiment with body oil. Pour a little oil on to the skin and let it run. Does it tickle? How does it feel? Does it have a smell? Use your hand to gently move the oil over the surface of the skin. Is it slippery? If the child is in agreement, try some gentle massage movements. This can be very calming, especially if you undertake this activity alongside playing gentle music. Experiment by using different kinds of soap and feeling bubbles on the skin.

EY   P+

Ideas using vibration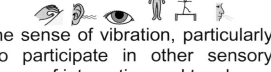

Some children enjoy the sense of vibration, particularly if they are unable to participate in other sensory activities involving a degree of interaction and touch.

Think about what vibrates within your home or setting. Children love feeling the sensation of placing bare feet in the door window of a washing machine while on a spin cycle. It is more fun if you spread a liquid soap and water on to the window first so that the children's feet slip off. Important: make sure the window is not hot.

Think about other types of vibration. Ask the child to hold the bowl for you while you use an electric mixer or allow the child to experience it for themselves. Experiment by using an old electric toothbrush to massage hands and feet using body oil or body lotion. Wrap the head of the toothbrush in different fabrics such as felt and fur. Use this to allow the child to feel the vibrations of different textures.

Add a little rice to a plastic container, wrap an elastic band around the container and ask the child to hold the container in both hands or hold it on a part of their body. Ping the elastic band. The child will feel the vibrations, hear the sound of the elastic band pinging and also hear and see the rice jumping.

Use a plastic or metal ruler and place it flat on a desk or worktop. Slide two-thirds of its length over the edge of the surface, hold it down with one hand and use your other hand to bend the plastic or metal down and release. This 'twangs' the ruler and creates good vibrations.

Ask two children to stretch a piece of string tightly between them. Pull and release the string quickly halfway along its length to create a vibration. Thread beads on to the string, do it again and watch the beads dance. Listen to the sound of the vibration; try shortening and lengthening the string. If you have them, try sitting a child on a large speaker or amplifier to feel the vibrations of music.

Equipment
Balloons/water/salt

Sienna is 6 years old. She has complex needs including a visual impairment, hearing impairment and is a wheelchair user.

She likes nothing more than being pushed over cobblestones while sitting in her chair. She loves the vibrations of the bumps, and squeals with excitement.

She has a large tricycle that is pulled by her dad's bike. She loves feeling the wind in her face and laughs when it is raining.

She enjoys the sensation of hot air being blown on her face and arms, and also enjoys sitting in front of a fan. Her mum has attached ribbons to the fan casing, which are blown over her skin.

Touch without touching

We tend to think that playing with touch involves bodily contact. In fact, the sensation of 'feeling' may not involve direct touch at all. We can: feel the breeze on our face; have the sense of being warm or cold; feel wet from the rain or feel spray when standing near to a waterfall or from splashy waves in the sea.

Consider how you can replicate these.

Replicating sensations

Tell the child a story where there is rain, wind and crashing waves. Replicate the kind of sensations they would feel if they were really there.

Blow up a balloon and squeeze the neck tight. Place the neck of the balloon near to a child's skin and let it go, allowing the air to blow against the child's skin. The sensation can be increased or decreased depending on how fast you let the air out. Add noise to the sensation by squeezing the neck of the balloon and let it make a sound when the air expels.

Experiment by pouring a little water into the balloon first. When the air expels it will also send out tiny droplets of water on to the skin.

Try experimenting by blowing through a straw and directing the air on to different parts of the body.

Play with a clean trigger spray bottle. Gently spray cold or warm water on to the body. To create a tingling sensation, spray cold water on to the child's arm or leg. Use a hairdryer to blow warm air on to the water. This will cause the water to evaporate, which creates a tingling sensation.

Try using sensory play to recreate a sensory experience. If you were standing by the sea with big crashing waves the water would taste salty. Try adding a little salt to the water in the trigger bottle and ask the child to taste the spray.

41

A sensory experience case study

Clay is very versatile and offers a wide range of sensory experiences. It changes between being wet and slippery and hard when baked or dried. It is possible to incorporate other sensory materials into clay. In the picture illustrated, Nyasha (aged 3) is using bits of foliage found in the garden to create 'hair' for her face.

This activity involved going out into the garden to see what we could find. It was a windy day, so Nyasha felt the breeze. We pushed our way past an evergreen tree to break off small pieces. The greenery brushed against her arms and face. She could smell the greenery, and the smell became stronger as she rubbed the leaves in her hands.

We went out in the early morning and Nyasha was excited to be 'smoking' like a dragon: blowing out steam in the cold air. She put her hand on the trunk of the tree, felt its roughness and compared it by running her fingers through the foliage, which was soft and smooth. Her hand became wet, as the tree was covered in morning dew.

Nyasha saw a spider's web covered in dew among the branches, and we blew gently on to the web and watched it vibrate. We watched the branches of the tree move in the wind, and Nyasha pretended to be a branch by swaying from side to side. We looked up into the tree and watched through the branches as the clouds moved across the sky.

Nyasha also wanted to recreate the tree by pushing 'branches' into clay. She decided how hard or soft she needed to push the foliage to make it stay in the soft clay. She blew on the creation to make the branches sway. Nyasha decided she wanted to water the tree, so we filled egg cups with water and dripped water on to the clay. She was fascinated by the change in the clay's texture and continued to play by creating 'mud' pictures using liquid clay. Such a simple play activity has a wealth of sensory benefit. Try it for yourself!

42

Chapter Three
Creating sensory play:
Playing with sight and vision

Throughout this book, we have advocated taking a child-centred approach, being aware of any sensitivities or underlying impairments. When considering activities that play with sight and vision, be aware of any visual impairment that a child may have, and work with them to make the best of the activity. This may mean you need to be aware of colour definition, placement of objects and the need for bright colours or brighter lighting.

Be aware of any particular sensitivity. We once worked with a child on the autism spectrum who could not abide anything bright red. This affected our planning. We worked with the child to adapt activities so that he could still participate.

Visual activities are synonymous with touch. If a child sees something, generally, they want to reach out for it. The majority of activities suggested will also have the touch symbol.

Using water and bubbles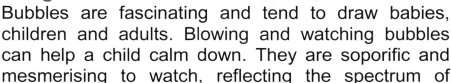
Bubbles are fascinating and tend to draw babies, children and adults. Blowing and watching bubbles can help a child calm down. They are soporific and mesmerising to watch, reflecting the spectrum of colours in the spheres produced.

Most children will want to participate in blowing and bursting bubbles, but remember that some children simply prefer to watch rather than participate, especially if the child has difficulty with fine motor skills such as manipulating hands and lips. Allow children the freedom to interact with the bubbles as they wish. Bubbles can be seen in many ways. Even watching bubbles in a fizzy drinks bottle can be relaxing.

Bubble pictures
Equipment
bowl/water/paint/
hypoallergenic liquid
detergent/ paint or printer
ink/silver foil/torch/straws

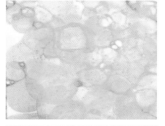

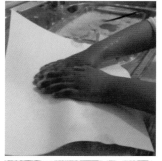

Bubbles come in many forms. Foam is made by crashing waves or small bubbles form and rise in a glass of fizzy drink. Be imaginative in your thinking.

The following ideas use bubbles that have been made from either hypoallergenic washing-up liquid or from baby 'no tears' shampoo. Occasionally, we have added liquid glycerine to the mix to make the bubbles stronger and they last longer. (This is not expensive and is available in small bottles from supermarkets. It is sold to add to royal icing to make it more pliable and so you will find it alongside the food colouring and icing sugar).

Making bubble pictures

Divide the mixture into several containers and add a little paint or colourant to each. Create bubbles by blowing into the mixture with a straw and then lay paper over the surface of the bubbles. Experiment by dipping the straw into the mixture, taking the straw out and blowing through it gently. Allow the bubble created to burst on the paper.

Making coloured bubbles 4-8 8+

We suggest doing this outside. Be careful that the colourant used will not stain. Coloured bubbles can be made easily by using strong natural food colouring or refill inkjet printer ink mixed into your solution. This is readily available from supermarkets, who often supply their own brands of refillable ink in small bottles more cheaply.

Be aware that this activity is very messy but it produces vibrant and interesting bubbles. Experiment by using these bubbles to print with, and try taking several prints, overlaying primary colours to create unique rainbow bubble images.

Try lining a container with silver foil. Pour in a little bubble solution and blow with a straw to create bubbles. The silver foil shines through the bubble solution and creates an 'unworldly' effect. Try shining a torch on the surface of the mixture.

44

Frozen bubbles Equipment
hypoallergenic liquid detergent/water/glycerine/ food colouring

Edible bubbles Equipment
Milkshake or desert whip/ glass/straw

Simple bubble tubes Equipment

clear plastic bottle/ coloured liquid soap/glitter

Try placing your hand into the bubble solution and create a circle using two fingers. Blow gently to create your own bubble. This also provides a further sense of 'cold' as the water evaporates from your hand. Create a bubble film by dipping your hand into the solution and running it across the top of a glass. Twist and turn the glass so that the natural light reflects on to the surface to create a rainbow.

Making frozen bubbles

Make up a strong batch of bubbles solution using 1 cup of water to a ½ cup of liquid detergent. Add in a few drops of glycerine to make a stronger solution and a few drops of colourant as desired.

Pour a little of the solution into a dish. Use a straw to blow some bubbles. Place the dish in the freezer and leave for 20-30 minutes (depending on your own freezer). Take the dish out carefully and the bubbles will be frozen. Experiment by touching them gently. Does the heat of a finger melt a bubble? Try pouring a few drops of water over the bubbles. What happens? Have they stayed the same shape, changed or disappeared?

Extra idea: making edible bubbles!

Create a thick milkshake using half a packet of desert whip. Pour into a glass and use a straw to blow bubbles. Once you have a good range of bubbles, put the whip in the freezer. It makes a delicious version of ice cream!

Making simple bubble tubes

Save up some empty large, clear plastic bottles. Fill them up using cheap, translucent coloured liquid detergent (the liquid can still be used, so you are not wasting it). Leave a small gap for an air bubble. Shake the bottle vigorously and turn it upside down so that the bubbles rise. They should rise slowly, as they are travelling through a viscous liquid.

Try adding small beads, glitter or shiny paper and foil to the bottle to create a more eye-catching effect.

45

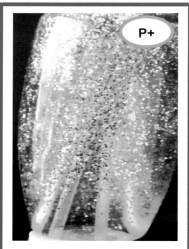

Glow stick bubble tube
Equipment
clean transparent plastic
bottle/coloured translucent
washing-up liquid/glitter/
glow sticks

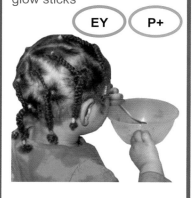

Traffic light jelly
3 packs of different colour
jelly/raisins/water/bowl/
torch/white paper/dark

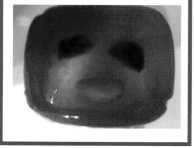

The same effect can be achieved using water and food colouring mixed with a little non-fungicidal wallpaper paste. The paste thickens the water so that it becomes more difficult for the bubbles to travel through it. The more viscous the water, the slower the bubbles or introduced objects will move.

Glow stick bubble tube

Try activating one or two glow sticks and adding them to a bottle filled with translucent washing-up liquid. Add a little glitter, take the bottle somewhere dark and watch the light of the glow stick reflect through the solution. Turn the bottle over and watch the bubbles travel slowly through the liquid and the glitter shine in the light! Glow sticks are easy to purchase and are inexpensive.

Using light and reflection

Playing with jelly

Jelly has lots of sensory play potential and is inexpensive. There is no need to purchase named brands; own brand labels are fine. We have tried these activities out with children aged as young as 2 years.

Making traffic light jelly

Mix 3 colours of jelly. Pour a little orange jelly into a container and put in the fridge. Leave until set. Add a layer of green followed by a layer of red (or whatever colours the child may like).

Making hidden faces

Once you have 2 layers which are set, add in some raisins or fruit to create a face before pouring over the final coloured layer. Experiment by adding other edible items between the layers. See if the children can guess what they are.

Try blindfolding the children and ask them to retrieve the hidden edible objects in the jelly, and then tell you what they think they taste like!

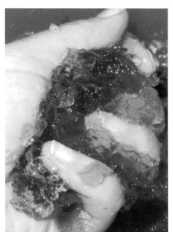

Making jelly Northern Lights

Turn the layered colour jelly out on to a plate and take into a dark room.

Place the jelly in front of a large piece of white paper, which will act as a projection screen. Shine a torch through the jelly.

To create the Northern Lights, move the plate gently to 'wobble' the jelly. The projected lights move and create amazing visual effects.

Experiment with different colours. Why not try making luminescent jelly? (see page 52).

Squelching jelly

There is nothing quite like squelching jelly between your fingers or even your toes!

Try making up a batch of jelly mix and pouring it into a large sand or water tray. Once set, allow the children to 'wade' in the jelly with their feet. Add some other textures such as rice or sand.

Once the jelly is broken up, try putting it in a glass and shining a torch through it.

Experiment by filling balloons with a jelly mix and let it set. Allow the children to feel the squidgy balloons.

Place some in a bowl and add warm water. Allow the children to feel the jelly melting. Once cold, this can become a drink.

Idea

Why not try making a fizzy jelly drink? Mix a packet of jelly using a little hot water and, instead of topping up with cold water, use lemonade, cola or another type of soft, fizzy drink.

47

Equipment
cellophane sweet
wrappers/cardboard
tubes/pen/laminated
pouches/laminator or
domestic iron.

**Colour a flower
Equipment**
white cut flower(s)/
natural food colouring/
water

Using cellophane sweet wrappers telescopes and projected images

At some point, most children will have picked up a tube to look through it like a telescope. In the illustrations we have expanded this idea using leftover sweet wrappers. Simply place coloured cellophane over the end of a tube and use an elastic band to secure in place.

Experiment by using two tubes together to create binoculars, each lens having a different coloured piece of cellophane. Three effects can be produced. Open either the left or right eye to see blue or yellow or open both eyes and the world changes to green.

Create a 'find the object' game by drawing something on to the cellophane that you have hidden within the setting. The children look through the telescope, see what they need to find, find it and bring it to you, at which point you simply change the cellophane with another image you have previously drawn and the game continues.

Sensory idea Expand this idea by using a torch. Push the cardboard tube on to the torch and seal any gap by using your hand or some tape. Turn on the beam and direct it towards a white or light-coloured wall or door. The image will be projected. Experiment with this idea and add different coloured cellophane to the tube. Try mixing and overlaying different colours.

Colour a flower

This particular activity works better with white flowers such as ox-eye daisies or white carnations. Add plenty of natural food colouring to a vase or container of water. Use a pair of scissors to cut the stem of the flower at a slant – this works better if the cut is made under warm water such as a running tap. Place the flower in the coloured water. As the flower draws the water up its stem, the colour of the flower will slowly change. Remember to smell the flowers.

Extension activity (if you are feeling clever!) Split the stem of the flower into two. Put each side into different coloured water and create a bi-coloured flower!

Kaleidoscope Equipment
photocopy templates/small cardboard tube/mirror card or highly reflective shiny card/holographic paper

Playing with optical illusions

Cut out thin strips of card each approximately 5mm wide. Place in a row 5mm apart as illustrated. Cut out two pieces of card for the top and bottom of the frame. Glue these on in order to create an optical grid. This can be used to create a strobe effect. Experiment by looking through the grid and moving it from left to right; it makes objects appear as though they are moving.

Now look through the grid at something that is moving. Get the children to move slowly for each other and take turns in looking through the grid. Talk to the children about what they see. Experiment further by shining a torch through the grid and projecting the image on to a wall or door. Try adding different coloured pieces of cellophane over the grid. What difference does this make? Do not do this activity if the child has epilepsy.

Making a kaleidoscope

Try making your own kaleidoscope. Use a small tube such as a cardboard roll found inside foil or food covering. Cut three pieces of mirror card the same length as the tube and tape them together, shiny side facing inwards, to create a long pyramid which will slide inside the tube and fit tightly (mirror card is available from most craft shops). A similar effect can be achieved using highly reflective shiny card.

Now, look through the tube at the metallic shiny paper (holographic wrapping paper works well). The image will be reflected several times by the mirror card, fragmenting the light. Turn the tube around in your hands while looking through it to add to the effect. Try looking at different objects.

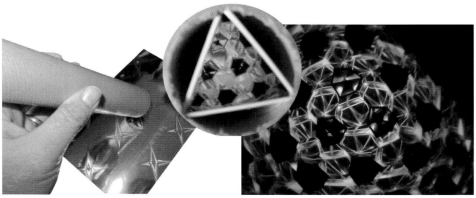

Equipment
Clear plastic water-filled bottle/glass bowl/torch/dark room/mirrors/sand

Looking through water

Experiment by using a simple clear plastic bottle full of water and see how images are distorted. Print out or draw some simple designs to experiment with. Roll the bottle across the image. Talk to the children about what they see. Is it what they expect? What has changed?

Try adding water to a round glass bowl. Take the bowl into a dark room and use a torch to shine light through the water on to the ceiling. Move the torch about under the bowl until the light breaks down the colour spectrum and a rainbow is projected on to the ceiling.

Try adding food colouring or inks. Does this make a difference? Try cutting out simple shapes from paper and laying them on the surface of the water. Do they project on to the ceiling?

Playing with reflective surfaces

Think about how else children can use reflections. Place a small mirror into the bowl of water. Look through the curved surface of the bowl into the mirror. Has the reflection been distorted?

The illustration below on the left uses small craft mirror stickers. Each small mirror has been mounted on to shiny paper. Ask the children to look into the mirrors. Because the tiles are separated, the image is fragmented. Children will see a Picasso-style image: an eye in one mirror; a nose in another. Try drawing the images that can be seen.

Experiment with sand or modelling clay. Use an object to impress a shape and look at it in a mirror. What has happened to the shape? Use your finger to draw in the sand and create faces. Ask the children to draw simple emotion faces and then ask them to replicate the expressions in the mirror.

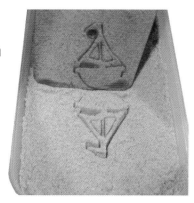

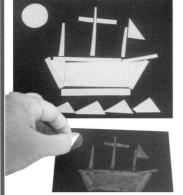

Making images touchable using sand

Cut out simple shapes from double-sided tape and stick on to black card. Pull the covering off to expose the sticky tape.

Place the picture on to a layer of play sand and push gently so that the sand sticks to the sticky tape. The sand will adhere to the tape, and sand pictures can be produced.

Sensory idea for older children

With older children, stick a sheet of double-sided tape on to card and carefully cut out shapes from the backing sheet.

Peel off the backing sheet to expose the sticky tape. Pour different coloured craft sand over the exposed area and shake off the remainder.

Continue exposing different areas, and build up a picture made of different coloured sand. If this is done on to thick card, boxes or pyramids can be created. Once completed, each picture can be varnished with water-based glue and left to dry. This adds more strength and ensures the sand does not fall off the card.

Creating tactile paints

Try adding fine sand to a mixture of paint and water-based glue. Once the painting has dried, it remains tactile to the touch. Try using other items to create textures. We suggest experimenting with torn-up kitchen roll, tissue paper, small polystyrene beads (available from craft shops) or use the filling from bean bags. Experiment by adding uncooked rice, confetti or pieces of wool. Ask the children for their own ideas.

Try gluing string on to a piece of card and painting over the top in order to create a tactile picture, or cut out shapes from card and stick them on to a backing sheet before painting. Why not add some scent to the mix for an extra sensory sensation?

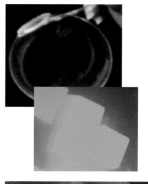

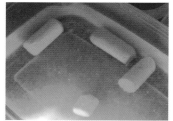

Playing with glow (needs adult supervision)

To create your own luminous glow paints, take a non-toxic ultraviolet reactive highlighter pen and place the nib in a small amount of water. Allow the ink to 'bleed' into the water. If you want to make a larger quantity, split the plastic outer casing of the pen and pull out the inner felt which stores the ink. Place this in the water and allow it to soak for a few minutes.

Store the solution in a small bottle and use a little at a time. You do not need much to create stunning effects.

We tried several colours and found that yellow and green fluorescent marker pens created the best effects.

The solution is fun on its own, but even more effective if looked at under ultraviolet lights. These can be purchased cheaply as strip lights or even small UV torches.

Ideas

Try mixing the solution with liquid soap to make luminescent bubbles. Add gelatine to the mixture to create glow in the dark soap cubes or use the glow in the dark water to make jellies and create your own luminescent Northern Lights.

Soak 2 or 3 white sticks of chalk in the solution overnight. Take them out and let them dry. Draw with the chalks on a dark surface and shine the ultraviolet light on to the drawing; it will glow in the dark.

Edible things that glow in the dark

Tonic water has a natural ability to glow blue in the dark under ultraviolet light. Experiment by making glow in the dark drinks or shaped ice cubes.

What about making luminescent glow in the dark edible jellies?

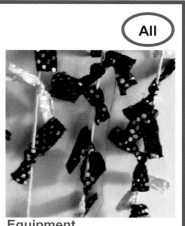

Equipment
pieces of shiny
fabric/string/plastic binder
or piece of wood or card to
hang mobile from

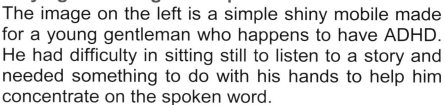

Playing with things that sparkle

The image on the left is a simple shiny mobile made for a young gentleman who happens to have ADHD. He had difficulty in sitting still to listen to a story and needed something to do with his hands to help him concentrate on the spoken word.

We made him a simple mobile using small strips of shiny fabric cut from a party dress. These were tied on to pieces of string and hung from a plastic slide binder. Using this simple tactile mobile he was able to sit through story times. He would run his fingers down the string and look at the shiny material. This made a huge difference to his normally disruptive behaviour.

Using a magnifier

We also provided him with a magnifying glass; this made a difference to his world. He was fascinated at seeing how things were constructed, including the fabric used in the mobile.

Try taking children outside on a hunt for small things such as sand, gravel, flowers, twigs, leaves or inspects. Encourage them to look at the items through a magnifying glass. Discuss what they can see. Ask the children to find more items to magnify. Some opticians are happy to give you old or sample lenses, which can be used as magnifiers.

Drawing faces on mirror glass using dry-wipe pens (or even Mum's make-up!)

Use a dry-wipe marker to draw outline faces on to a mirror. Play a game where the child looks in the mirror and tries to make the same expression that they have drawn. Tell a story, and ask the children to make a face representing the characters' emotions.

Draw a simple face on to the mirror using dry-wipe markers and allow the child to 'make up' the image using cheap cosmetic make-up. When finished, wipe off and start again.

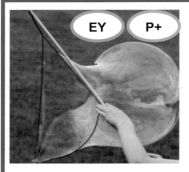

Equipment
2 bamboo canes or long sticks/string/6 cups of water (distilled works well, but you can use tap water)/½ cup of strong washing-up liquid/ ½ cup of cornflour (optional)/½ cup of baking powder (optional)/
1 tablespoon glycerine/colourant (optional)

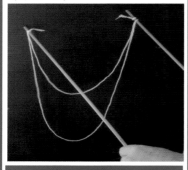

Instructions
Cut a length of string approximately 1 metre long. Cut a second length approximately 1.5 metres long. Tie them together at both ends and tie each end to a separate cane.

(You can use a hula hoop for a bubble wand if your bubble solution is in a sufficiently large tray).

Mix all the ingredients together in a large bucket. Stir it very well.

Dip in your bubble wand. Lift it out of the solution, open up the canes and gently swing the wand in a circle to create a giant bubble!

A sensory experience case study

Casey is 8 years old. He was diagnosed with autism and dyspraxia when he was 3.

The world for Casey is a confusing place. He finds it hard to socialise with others, especially when it comes to sharing and taking turns.

He prefers not to look at you when he is talking to you, but instead looks either at the ground or just to one side.

Everything he does has to be perfect. If it is not 'just so' then it gets destroyed. If he draws a picture that does not look exactly like the one he is copying, he will tear it up in frustration. This is due to his literal thinking and understanding. Sadly, Casey's self-esteem and confidence are low because he puts himself under pressure to get things right.

Casey's key worker recognised this and decided to introduce him to some sensory play opportunities that did not require a 'finished product'; the enjoyment of the activity was the play in itself.

Casey was introduced to bubbles. He had played with them before but had never made his own bubble solution adding glycerine, baking powder and cornflour.

Once he had made the solution and bubble wand he went outside to try it out. It was fantastic; he was able to create amazing, huge bubbles! There was no need to complete a finished article; making the bubbles themselves was the activity. There was no pressure.

During the activity, his communication increased, he wanted others to see his achievement, and his self-esteem and confidence improved. His key worker took photographs of the bubbles he had made and displayed them in the setting. He was proud to show the pictures to other children and his parents.

54

Chapter Four
Creating sensory play:
Playing with sound

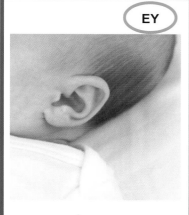

EY

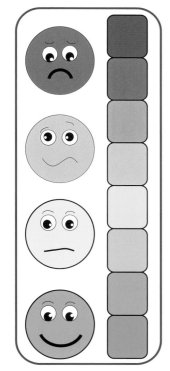

This template is available in our photocopy resource pages.

photocopy

Much of our world is driven by sound. We are surrounded by it all the time and tend to block out the sounds that are unimportant to us, concentrating instead on the bits of sound we need to know about such as a voice.

Have you ever walked into a quiet room or area and breathed a sigh of relief, recognising that your senses have been bombarded with sound even though you were not particularly aware of it at the time?

Many children are sound sensitive. Be aware of any sensitivity and only introduce one sound at a time. If the child shows any signs of distress then either reduce the noise level or stop until the child is able to continue.

Using our voices and bodies
We have a lot of ability to make noises using nothing but our own bodies. Start off by asking the children what kind of sounds their voices can make from the tiniest whisper to the loudest shout.

Make a noise-o-meter (or use the template provided on page 94). Ask the children to point at a face, based on the volume of noise made. Ask the children to make the judgement regarding the noise level: green being fine and red being too noisy.

Extend this activity by experimenting with other sounds that can be made by the mouth such as clicking your tongue, whistling, blowing raspberries and anything else the children can think of. Develop this to imitate animal and bird sounds such as a duck quacking, a dog barking or a donkey braying. There are many songs to use to complement this activity such as 'Old McDonald had a Farm'.

55

Build on this idea of making noises by using your body instead of your mouth. Experiment by asking the children to make the noise of various animal footsteps such as a mouse or an elephant.

Encourage the children to use more than just their feet. Tap fingers on a table to represent a mouse, slide one hand across another to represent a snail or slap hands on thighs to represent flapping of wings.

Build the children's imaginations by telling a short story of a group of animals taking a journey. Ask them to create the sound effects using just their bodies. Try to include actions representing the environment, such as walking through mud, water or long grass.

Enhancing voices: making megaphones and microphones

The most obvious item to use to create a megaphone is a cardboard tube. These are quick, easy and fun to use, and can be decorated and personalised. Try using different lengths of tube. Does it make a difference to how the voice sounds? Try making quiet or loud sounds.

To make a microphone that amplifies sound, use a cardboard or plastic cone. Large yoghurt pots also work well for this activity. Cut off the smallest end of the yoghurt pot, making a cone shape. Cut a balloon in half and stretch it over the larger end of the cone. Add a little tape to secure it. Try speaking into the open end of the cone. The sound waves created by your voice will hit the balloon, will vibrate, and will be bounced back, amplifying the sound. It works well as a simple microphone.

Try pinching the centre of the balloon with two fingers, lifting it and letting it go. The balloon will snap back down, creating a sound that is amplified by the cone. Beware, this can be quite loud!

Megaphones Equipment
cardboard/plastic cone or large yoghurt pot/balloons/scissors

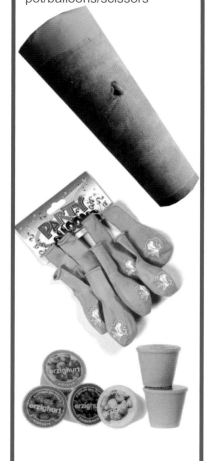

Making more sounds using balloons
Finger sounds

Balloons are inexpensive, readily available and have far more value than just blowing them up for decoration! This idea uses small balloons. Balloons sold for water bombs are just the right size for small fingers.

Stretch out the neck of a balloon and add something to make a sound such as rice, a small bell, a little water or small buttons. Blow up the balloon and make sure you tie the knot as close to the body of the balloon as possible.

The rest of the balloon neck is used to stretch over children's fingers so that when they move their fingers the balloons will make a noise. Try creating a balloon orchestra with several children participating. They need to be 'conducted' and remember which sound is on which finger.

EY **P+**

Finger sound balloons
Equipment
packet of small balloons/permanent marker (if you wish to draw faces)/ingredients to add to balloons to make sounds

Sound pairs

Expand this idea by playing a game of pairs. All the balloons are put on to a tray or the floor. One child picks up a balloon and shakes it. They then pick up another balloon and if the sound matches they take the pair. If not, the next child has a go and has to remember the sound the balloon makes to know which balloons make the pairs. If the balloons are only partially inflated, this game can also be played by feeling the objects in the balloons.

This can also be done by using different items in small pots or containers.

Listening game

Use the same balloons to create sounds. For each sound, ask the children to make a particular movement, for example, hands in the air, hop up and down or even hula hoop. Place the balloons into a bucket or bag. Randomly take out a balloon and shake it. The children need to remember the correct movement against the sound heard.

Happy Families sound games
Equipment
various ingredients to make 'sound families' e.g. beans, lentils, rice, couscous/small balloons or small containers

Happy Families sound games

Create a range of different sounds by placing objects into small containers or balloons. The children need to 'collect' sounds as they would collect family members in a game of Happy Families.

Consider what you can use to make different types of family sounds such as a 'dry food family' (rice, pasta or lentils) or a 'metallic family' (paper clips, metal buttons or coins).

Deal out 4 containers to each child. Ask them to listen hard to the kinds of sounds being made and give them 4 'sound family' names. The children take turns to ask if anyone has 'a dry food family member'. If so, they then swap it with a container or balloon they do not want. The winner is the first child to make up their entire sound family.

Distorting sound

Ask someone to speak to you. Put your hands over your ears and tap quickly. The sound becomes distorted in a similar way to looking at an object through a strobe light. You only have partial hearing. Experiment with the children by playing them different sounds while they are tapping their ears. Can they recognise the various sounds?

Sound bingo

Create a simple bingo sheet of animals. Download free animal sounds from the internet, play them to the children, make the sounds yourself or ask a child to make the sounds for you. Ask the children to cross off the animals they have heard until you have a winner.

Expand this activity by asking the children to draw or write down the names of the animals that they have heard in order to create their own bingo cards.

Add in some stray sounds associated with the animal rather than being the voice of the animal, for example, the sound of a horse's hooves galloping rather than a 'neigh'.

58

Whisper game
Equipment
prepared sentences

Home-made telephones
Equipment
yoghurt pots, paper cups or tin cans/string

Whisper game

Sit the children in a circle and explain that when the child hears something they cannot ask what has been said again and can only pass what they hear on to the next person passing the message around the circle. The last person to receive the message says it out loud and sees if the message has been distorted on the way around the circle.

A variation on this theme is to send around the circle a sequence of noise in tongue clicks similar to Morse code. See if the sequence has changed on the way round. This requires sustained concentration and is not suitable for all children. How can you adapt this idea to create other listening challenges?

Home-made telephones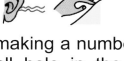

Vary the game above by making a number of simple telephones. Make a small hole in the base of a yoghurt pot, tin, paper cup or other suitable container. Knot a piece of string and thread the end of the string through the hole. Do the same with the opposite end of the string so that you have two containers connected by string.

Initially, get the children to have a conversation with each other through their telephone. One child speaks into their pot while the next child, who is standing a distance away, listens to the sound by placing their 'receiver' over their ear. Note that the string attaching the two pots needs to be taut in order to allow the sound to travel well.

Once the children have experimented, place them in a circle, each holding a receiver and a speaker in each hand. The message is then sent around the group, with each child using their own telecommunication system to receive and transmit messages.

Try using a long hose pipe or tube with a funnel on either end. Speak into one end and listen to the other.

59

Vuvuzela Equipment
cardboard cone/cardboard tube (to fit snugly in cone)/straw (optional)/ balloon/scissors

Keiran decorated his vuvuzela with soft fleece so that it was soft to touch. He decided it was how pirates were called in to dinner.

EY   P+

Creating instruments you blow

Vuvuzela (warning: this can be very loud!)

To create a simple vuvuzela you will need a sturdy cardboard or plastic cone. If you do not have access to these, they can be made easily by rolling a piece of card diagonally, taping it in shape and then cutting off the base and top so that they are straight.

You will also need a cardboard tube that fits snugly into the smaller end of the cone. Again, this can be achieved by rolling up card, placing it in the cone and letting it expand to fill the hole. Tape the card in order to create a strong tube. The inside tube from food covering, foil or kitchen rolls also works well.

It is important to ensure that the cardboard tube is inserted into the cone with no gaps. If there are any gaps, then the air can escape and the vuvuzela will not sound.

Create a small hole in the cone to blow through. If you are making one between several children, give each child a piece of straw to insert into this hole so that they each have their own mouthpiece, which is more hygienic and can be thrown away.

Lastly, cut off the neck of a balloon. Stretch the balloon tightly over the large end of the cone and tape it in place. Push the tube into the cone so that it touches the balloon. It is essential that it touches the balloon or the instrument will not work.

Now blow into the hole (or straw). The air pushed into the cone wants to escape. It will hit the balloon, expand it slightly and send the air down the tube, vibrating as it goes. The noise created can be very loud! For deeper sounds, lengthen the tube used; for higher-pitched sounds, shorten the tube.

Try experimenting by making large and small vuvuzelas. Be aware of any children who are sensitive to noise.

Straw recorders
Equipment
large straws (ones from fast food restaurants work well)/scissors

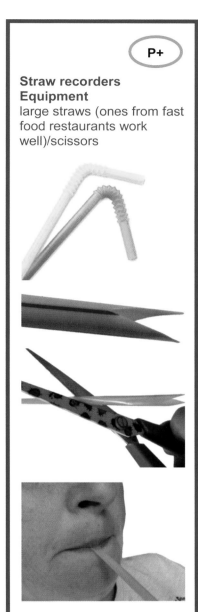

Pipe fifes
Equipment
plastic pipe or Perspex tube approx 2cm in diameter/drill to make holes/items for decoration

Straw recorders

Noise is created by vibrating air. The activity does this by creating a double reed similar to the reeds found on a bassoon or oboe. It works better with very large straws such as those from fast food outlets.

Cut the end of the straw into a point. Firmly press down on both sides so that the straw is flattened. Place the point between your lips and blow gently. Allow the 'reed' to vibrate and send the sound down the straw.

Things to know

If the straw if squeezed too tightly between your lips the air will not enter the straw and no sound will be made. If the straw is cut at too shallow an angle the two sides will not be long enough to vibrate. Some children find this activity very easy and others will have difficulty blowing the straw. We recommend that you try it out for yourself first of all so that you are able to advise the children. Once you have the technique you can expand the activity.

Try making the straw shorter and the sound will rise in tone. Push two straws together to extend the length and the tone will lower. Experiment by making one or two very small holes in the straw to put your fingers over (like holes in a recorder). Blow into the straw and lift your fingers on and off the holes in order to create a range of different pitches.

Expanding the idea by creating a fife

Use a plastic tube (plumbers' tube is easily accessible from DIY shops and is inexpensive) and initially drill a mouthpiece hole. Block the end of the tube nearest the mouthpiece with a cork or some clay. Blow across the top of the hole (as you would to make a sound from a bottle). Once you achieved a sound, drill several more holes along the length of the tube. By covering the various holes you will vary the pitch and create a flute-like musical instrument. Note that the hole you blow into needs to be slightly larger than the finger holes.

Tube kazoo
Equipment
cardboard roll/tissue paper/single hole punch (or use the sharp end of a pencil)/elastic band

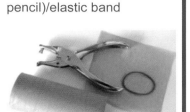

Card kazoo
Equipment
card/scissors/elastic bands/straw

Making a kazoo

A kazoo works by using the sound of your voice through humming rather than creating a new sound. There are various ways of making kazoos. Try these two ideas and experiment for yourself.

Tube kazoo

Very simple kazoos can be created by using a small cardboard tube, such as a tube from the inside of a toilet roll or kitchen roll. Make a small hole in the side of the tube (single hole punches can be purchased cheaply from craft stores or supervise the use of a sharp pencil to make the hole). Decorate your tube, but make sure you don't cover the hole.

Place a single sheet of tissue paper over the end of the tube and secure with an elastic band. Place your mouth to the hole and loudly hum a tune. The sound vibrates on to the tissue paper and becomes distorted.

Card kazoo

Cut two pieces of thick card 12cm x 3cm (corrugated box card works well). Cut it so that the corrugations run down the long side of the card.

Place a thick elastic band over one piece of card from end to end. Cut two 3cm long pieces of straw and place one under the elastic band 2cm from the end of the card. Place the second **OVER** the elastic band. Now use the second piece of card, and sandwich the elastic band and straws together. Use the two smaller elastic bands to secure both ends of the kazoo. Now place the side of the kazoo to your mouth and hum a tune. By squeezing the card together you can alter the pitch of the hum.

Decorate your kazoo. Remember that if you are using water-based paints the colour will come off on your lips. Use permanent markers or stickers. We used shiny pipe cleaners to decorate ours. This kazoo can also be made using wide wooden lolly sticks instead of card. This makes a sturdier instrument. The vibration of the card also tickles your lips.

Wind chimes

Wind chimes
Equipment
various objects to make noise/string/hanger

Wind chimes are easy to make and at very little cost, but are very effective for sensory play. Take a look around your setting or home. What makes a noise when gently knocked together?

What about:
- metal cutlery, knives, forks and spoons
- keys, shells, bells
- washed empty drink cans
- small flower pots
- small stones or pebbles
- tops of jam jars
- metal bottle tops from beer bottles (ask at your local pub)

or for more musical chimes:
- bars from a xylophone
- hollow bamboo sticks
- different lengths of copper pipe

Or how about making your own chimes from air-drying clay? Effective chimes can be made by rolling out a thin piece of clay and cutting it into different lengths. Make a single hole near to the top of each length and roll the clay around a rolled-up piece of card, pencil or other cylindrical shape. Seal the seam by gently squeezing together and using a little clay mixed with water.

Once dry, slide the clay from the cylinder and attach to the mobile hanger using lengths of string. Other effective clay shapes can be created by using a shaped cutter. Always remember to add a hole for hanging before the clay dries.

Consider what you can use for your mobile hanger. Suggestions include: wire hangers; CDs; picture frames; colanders; driftwood; and a ruler. The list is endless and it is up to you and the children to decide what is available to you. Some supervision and help may be required during this activity.

EY   P+

63

Rain sticks

Rain sticks
Equipment
long cardboard tube/2 paper circles/2 rubber bands/silver foil/handful of rice

Very simple and effective rain sticks can be created by just using a long cardboard tube, some silver foil or newspaper, two pieces of paper, a handful of rice and two elastic bands.

Seal off one end of the tube using the paper and the elastic band. Take either the silver foil or the newspaper and loosely scrunch it up and feed it into the tube. Carry on until the tube is filled. Pour in your rice, and seal the open end of the tube with the remaining paper and elastic band.

When the tube is turned over, the rice needs to find its way down through the paper or tin foil by gravity. It will make the sound of rain while travelling down the tube. Note: If the rice slides down the tube too quickly the paper or foil is not scrunched sufficiently; if the rice does not travel down the tube, the paper or foil is scrunched and packed too tightly. Experiment until you have it right. Decorate your rain stick.

Another way to create the noise of rain is to create a tube using corrugated paper or card. Seal the seam with tape. Seal one end of the tube with paper and an elastic band, add a handful of rice and seal the other end. Place the tube on to a table or the floor. Slowly roll the tube along. The rice will fall from one corrugation to the next, creating the sound of rain. Try rolling the tube on a sloping surface; the rain will fall by itself. Expand this idea by trying different things inside the tubes such as paper clips, pasta, buttons, shells or stones.

Elastic band sound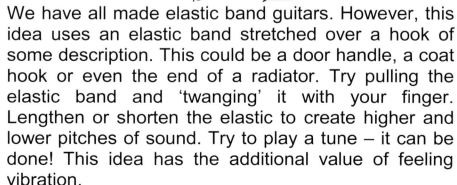

We have all made elastic band guitars. However, this idea uses an elastic band stretched over a hook of some description. This could be a door handle, a coat hook or even the end of a radiator. Try pulling the elastic band and 'twanging' it with your finger. Lengthen or shorten the elastic to create higher and lower pitches of sound. Try to play a tune – it can be done! This idea has the additional value of feeling vibration.

Paint by sound

Small bells can be purchased cheaply from craft shops. Thread a series of bells on to a string or pipe cleaners and attach them securely on to the end of several paintbrushes.

See if the children can identify the different colours by listening to the number of bells on each brush, for example, red = 2 bells, blue = 3 bells, green = 5 bells.

Musical paints

Fill some clear glass jars with different coloured paint; each jar needs a different level of liquid. Ask the child to tap the jar with the wooden end of their paintbrush and listen to the sound it makes. Ask the children to put the jars into order from the highest to the lowest sound.

For older children, help them to tap out a nursery rhyme or well-known tune. Get the children to 'paint' a song, by dabbing the colour of paint on to paper to represent which jar they hit in which order so as to recreate the song.

Creating works of art from sounds

Take the children out on a sound walk. Listen carefully to everything they hear, and write it down.

Talk to the children about the kinds of sounds they heard and how they could be represented in paint, for example, the sound of the wind through the trees might be represented by a brush stroke of green or blue paint, the sound of a fire engine might be a series of red zig zags or the bray of a donkey might be represented by a dot and a dash for the 'eeyore'.

It is up to the children to experiment with how they think that the sounds could be visualised. They may wish to use other items to create a collage. This activity produces some very interesting artwork!

Creating sound effects

Jason is 10 years old. He had an accident when he was 8, leaving him with a brain injury, resulting in a learning impairment, a short attention span and a sensitivity to noise. Often, Jason craves quiet places and holds his hands over his ears when the surrounding noise gets too much for him.

Jason's teaching assistant, Becky, supports him by reading to him quietly, offering lots of visual structure and things to hold and touch.

One day, during the story, Becky asked Jason what kind of sound stars would make if they could. She was very pleased when Jason picked up a triangle and played it, making a small, gentle 'ting'.

Becky began to experiment, asking Jason to help her collect a box together of all the sounds they would need for a story. Becky read the story and involved Jason in looking for items.

In addition to the triangle, they added a pen to click to represent a hopping bird, and a book where the pages could be flipped to represent the bird's wings. Jason could also feel the breeze by flipping the pages of the book near to his skin. Also, Jason was involved in making his own sounds. He used his voice to represent the waves coming into shore by saying 'shhhhhhh, shhhhhhh'.

His mum was invited into the school at the end of the following day for story time. She was delighted to see that Jason was sitting up the front with Becky. As Becky read the story to the rest of the class, Jason was making the sound effects.

Jason could not read out loud. However, he was very proud of his achievement. Through his involvement in sound effects, his peers were able to praise him and tell him they liked what he had done. **How can you challenge children to make a sound effects box for a story?**

66

Chapter Five
Creating sensory play:
Playing with taste

Eating lemons!

Taste and smell are closely linked; they are the two senses that define if something is safe to eat or not. Babies and young children begin to discover the world by putting things into their mouths.

Our lips and tongues are very sensitive, and the average human has about 10,000 taste buds. They are not all on the tongue: some are under the tongue; some are on the inside of the cheeks; some are on the roof of the mouth. Some can even be found on the lips; these are especially sensitive to salt.

The illustration here shows how Rutendo, aged 2, reacts when she tastes a piece of lemon for the first time. Note in the last picture of the sequence that she is still going back for more. She knows it won't harm her as she trusts the adult who gave it to her and she wants to try again – perhaps to see if it is the same the second time around!

Taste is very individual. People will have strong opinions on whether they like something or not. Children will also respond differently to the sensation of hot or cold. Taste can differ when using different temperatures for the same ingredients, for example, hot or cold custard.

Also, consider the textures you are introducing. Some children may have an aversion to particular textures such as sloppy foods (porridge) or hard foods (celery).

Be aware of any allergies or intolerances; seek approval from parents if the child is not your own. Finally, be aware of hygiene. Ensure children wash their hands before and after activities.

Considering textures

Playing with food is fun, and children are often more interested in the activity if they think they can eat it.

Introduce a range of food and drink, and ask the children to help identify the textures of various foods. Create a sensory chart of likes and dislikes.

Liquids can be of various viscosities: compare water to fruit juice, fruit juice to drinkable yoghurt, drinkable yoghurt to thick milkshakes. See what you have available to use in your setting.

Semi-solid comparisons might include soft textures such as porridge, jellies, ice cream or soft cheese.
Crunchy loose solids may include cereals, crisps, toast or crackers.
Loose, easy to eat foods include foods such as cooked rice or pasta.
Easy to bite foods include fruit such as apple pieces, bananas, plums or cooked food such as bread and biscuits.
Chewy food may include toffees and sweets.
Hard food requiring the ability to bite may include carrot sticks or celery.

Try making foods that have the same texture but taste different, for example, mashed potatoes, mashed swede or how about mashed beetroot?

Take a taste

In addition to trying out textures, ask the children about the tastes of the food. Sort various bowls of food into taste receptor piles, including bitter, sour, salty and sweet. Explore the different types of sensations you get when tasting food. Try a little sherbet to find a taste that is also fizzy. Experiment with still and sparkling water. Experiment by adding two tastes together such as sweet and sour.

Create an edible necklace by threading various foods on to a string. Some breakfast cereals are good for this activity.

EY P+

Experiment with different types of foods and record children's reactions and preferences.

68

All

Experimenting with bananas
Equipment
bananas/masher/knife/oven/freezer/lolly sticks

Changing tastes and textures

Many foods have the ability to change in taste, texture, look and smell depending on how we cook them. Consider how you can use and expand these ideas for other food types.

Let's go bananas!

Start by asking the child what a banana looks like, feels like, smells like and tastes like. Does it change if it is a new green banana or an old yellow banana where the skin is starting to turn brown?

Try mashing a banana and compare the texture, taste, look and smell. Try spreading it on toast and putting it under the grill. Bake a banana in the oven in its skin for 10 minutes at 180 degrees Celsius until it is brown. Carefully open the banana with a knife, as it will be very hot. Ask the child the same questions and compare the results.

Try cutting a banana into very thin slices. Put them on to a baking tray and place in the oven on a very low temperature. Let the banana slices dry out and become crisp. Again, compare the results.

Experiment by cutting the banana into chunks, pushing in a lolly stick and putting it in the freezer to make banana popsicles. Even better if you cover them in chocolate!

Other food that changes

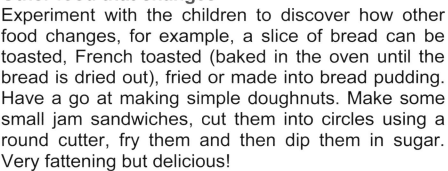

Experiment with the children to discover how other food changes, for example, a slice of bread can be toasted, French toasted (baked in the oven until the bread is dried out), fried or made into bread pudding. Have a go at making simple doughnuts. Make some small jam sandwiches, cut them into circles using a round cutter, fry them and then dip them in sugar. Very fattening but delicious!

What about the simple sultana? Try soaking them in fruit juice to make them plump and sweet or putting them in the freezer to create a refreshing frozen treat.

Peanut butter play dough
Ingredients
1 cup of powdered milk
½ cup of peanut butter
(crunchy for added texture
or smooth)
1 teaspoon of honey

Oat play dough
Ingredients
1 cup of flour
2 cups of oatmeal
1 cup of water

Chocolate play dough
Ingredients
3 cups of icing sugar
6 tablespoons of cocoa
powder
¾ cup of powdered milk
(may need more)
½ cup of butter at room
temperature (no
substitutes)
½ cup of light corn syrup
1 teaspoon of vanilla
All ingredients are available
from supermarkets.

Edible play dough

These are fun and exciting activities to do with children. All of the recipes can be baked but they are also safe to eat raw.

Peanut butter play dough*allergy alert

This is a very simple mix using honey, powdered milk and smooth peanut butter (or use crunchy if you want to make a textured dough). The recipe provided makes about one cup of dough.

Add all the ingredients together in a bowl and mix (very simple and easy to do with children). If the children wish, add different food colourings so that they can make small edible models. Models made from this recipe can be cooked for 10 minutes at 180 degrees Celsius to make little biscuits or they can be eaten raw.

Oat play dough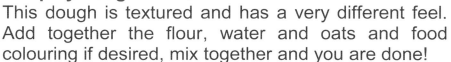

This dough is textured and has a very different feel. Add together the flour, water and oats and food colouring if desired, mix together and you are done!

Again, this recipe can be baked as above. If you want to add sweeter flavours, add a little honey or sugar.

Chocolate play dough

This dough smells and tastes of chocolate and is great to model with. Combine all the ingredients in a bowl. Mix and knead together until all the ingredients bind.

Knead the dough on a clean surface until it becomes smooth and stretchy. It should lose its stickiness at this stage. If it is still sticky add a little more powdered milk or if too crumbly add a little water.

Again, this recipe can be baked as above to create small biscuits but is safe to eat raw.

Food modelling Equipment

various foods such as strawberries, grapes, potatoes, celery, peppers, sultanas/small knife/cocktail sticks or straws

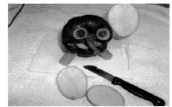

Food modelling

Children enjoy this activity; we have just provided a few ideas, but allow the children to be creative and freely experiment.

Be aware that the children will be using a range of tools to cut, slice or join together various foodstuffs with cocktail sticks. Supervision is required for younger children.

Simple crocodile

Abby, who created this crocodile, used strawberries, grapes, sultanas and a little celery. They were joined together using pieces of cocktail sticks. (Abby also decided the crocodile needed more than four feet!)

Two grapes were used as eyes along with two sultanas for the pupils. She felt it needed a tail, so leaves were added from a piece of celery.

Have a look at the pictures and work out how the food models were constructed. You are only limited by your own imagination. Help the children to think about how they could cut, shape and construct the models they wish to create and what food stuffs would be best to use.

Also, have a try at creating food pictures, where food is simply laid out on a plate. These are simpler for some children, especially those who have issues with fine motor skills.

Jelly play
Equipment
packet of unflavoured gelatine/various flavourings

(All)

Jelly play

Earlier in the book, we suggested using jellies in visual and touch play.

These are few ideas to play with taste by using gelatine as the binding ingredient to hold in flavours. Jelly is a good way of introducing very young children to new flavours. Be aware that some gelatine includes animal products; vegetarian gelatine is also available from supermarkets.

Unflavoured gelatine can be purchased cheaply from most supermarkets. Begin by reading the instructions on the packet; not all gelatines are made in the same way.

Consider what can be incorporated into clear, tasteless jelly. Some substances will colour the jelly and others will remain transparent. Begin by adding a few drops of simple flavoured essences such as banana, vanilla, peppermint or lemon. Ask the children to smell the jelly, guess the flavour and then take a taste.

Items can be added to the mix to help the children decide what flavour they might be tasting such as a piece of banana or a peppermint leaf (easily grown or purchased from a supermarket).

Take a look around your setting or home. What else do you have to flavour jelly? Think about what dissolves in water: tea, coffee, gravy powder or even cheese sauce mix. Other items can be suspended in the mix such as spices and herbs. Experiment and broaden your ideas. Remember that jelly does not always have to be sweet.

Provide a range of ingredients for the children to experiment with. Some will be accepted and others rejected. Offer the children various food colourings and explore expectations such as red jelly tasting of strawberries when in fact it tastes of oranges!

Grow your own indoor herb gardens

There is lots of sensory benefit in bringing nature indoors and growing your own plants. Not only can you pick and taste the fruits of your labours but you can touch, smell and see the plants growing.

Seeing a plant grow through the care given by a child can help to raise self-esteem and confidence. Children are proud of their achievements, especially if they can be seen and appreciated by others.

Additionally, herbs can be dried and used in a wide variety of sensory play projects. Seeds can be gathered and stored, and fresh herbs can be eaten directly from the plant.

Take a look around your setting for appropriate containers in which to grow plants. They do not necessarily need to be in pots; take a look in your lost property box. What about growing plants in a pair of boots or shoes, an old lunchbox or a pencil case? Perhaps the children could bring something in from home. Anything that will hold some soil and water can be used.

Cress seeds are cheap, readily available and will sprout on simple beds of damp cotton wool or even damp newspaper. Encourage creativity by getting the children to make their own cress beds. Simple items such as yoghurt pots or egg shells make good containers. Easy-to-grow indoor herbs that have a strong scent or taste include:

Basil – likes lots of sun and warmth
Chives – happy to grow anywhere, but needs light
Parsley – likes full sun
Rosemary – a strong scent and flavour; likes the sun
Thyme – grows well from a cutting

Get the children to crush the leaves in their hands, smell, taste and identify the different herbs.

Aversion to food

Many children have aversions to particular foods or cannot eat specific things due to intolerances such as gluten, wheat or dairy products.

Benjamin had a different aversion: he would not eat anything unless it was green. He happily ate cabbage, green beans and peas, but would not touch other foods such as bread, butter and milk.

His parents were desperate. They began using food colouring in everyday ingredients such as milk, and made their own green cakes and bread. This worked, and Ben was able to increase his food intake. However, it was not going to solve the problem altogether, especially if he went elsewhere for a meal.

Mealtimes were horrendous, with food being thrown across the room. Mum decided to inject some humour by creating pictures and models from the food on Ben's plate. She also developed food-based activities and games that he would enjoy, particularly in relation to counting. Additionally, she purchased a hand puppet that sat down to meals with them. The puppet 'ate' the various foods that were not green in order to encourage Ben to do the same.

Ben became interested to see what he was going to have for dinner but still ate very little and picked out the green items.

One day, his mum was out shopping and discovered a pair of green-tinted sunglasses. These were duly purchased and given to Ben. He was fascinated with these and would not take them off.

Ben's mum looked for a range of 'white' foods that would look green through his glasses to see what would happen. These included cauliflower, potatoes, bread, fish and eggs. She also continued creating 'playful' meals to encourage Ben to sit at the table.

Over time, Ben's eating habits improved. Once he decided that he liked the taste of food that had been dyed or tinted green by his glasses, he was more willing to try it without them on. His diet was still limited but at least he had begun to eat a more balanced diet.

Chapter Six
Creating sensory play:
Playing with smell

The sense of smell is something we don't often think about until something happens that makes us sit up and recognise there is a smell we either like, don't like or may even worry about such as the smell of smoke.

For some children, however, their sense of smell is overpowering and is prioritised in the brain before other senses.

It is often difficult for us to distinguish one smell from another when they are all around us. Have you ever been near to a perfume counter in a shop? To some people, all the various scents eventually flow into one and it is hard to know which you like best.

Supermarkets recognise the power of smell by filtering the scent of freshly baking bread through the air ducts. You are given 'smells' to encourage you to buy.

Different people will feel that the same thing has a strong or a weak aroma. Remember this when working with individual children. Some will require less fragrance and others more.

Some of the activities suggested in this chapter use a heat source to enhance smells. Be aware of using heat sources with younger children or children who do not understand the consequences of touching something hot.

We also suggest a range of unusual smells that children may or may not like. Try the ideas and see what works for you! Also be aware of the other activities suggested in this book which also use the sense of smell, particularly those in the previous chapter, 'Playing with taste'.

Smell that picture (P+)
Equipment
magazines/books/scissors/
paper/glue/items from
around the setting

Smell that picture

Provide the children with several magazines and some scissors. Ask them to cut out of the magazine pictures of things that smell, such as lemons, flowers, or a jar of coffee.

Identify several items that you may have around the setting or home which match the pictures. Blindfold the children and ask them to smell what you have given them. Some children may also wish to touch the object. Ask the children to look at the pictures again and identify the smell they have just encountered.

Going for a smelly walk

Again, look for pictures that can be cut out of a magazine or book representing things that you might smell in your local community or in your own setting.

This may include leaves, flowers, horses, dogs, wood, grass, cars, perfume, and the sea – whatever is local to you. Create a checklist of what the child has smelled while out on a walk and tick them off. Add new scents to the list as you walk along.

Painting by smells

Add some perfume to different coloured paints. Work with the children so that they can identify the colour by the smell. Make each smell distinctive. Think about what else you can add that smells, such as herbs and spices.

Some children prefer smells that remind them of colours, for example, strawberry or cherry smell for red, banana smell for yellow, oranges for orange, and coffee for brown.

Paint blocks of individual colour on different sheets of paper. Once dry, ask the child to close their eyes and identify the colour of the paint from its smell. If the paint does not smell particularly strong, try scratching it with your fingernail.

Nice and nasty smell game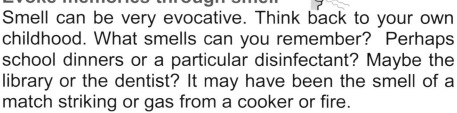

When we think of games involving smell we often limit ourselves to things we find in the kitchen. Expand this by working with the children to gather together all sorts of things that smell. We have suggested some items, but keep an open mind and allow the children to gather items available within the setting.

Old books, newly printed magazines, rubber bands, furniture polish, a handful of coins and a bank note, rubber mats, grass mats, felt pens, whiteboard markers and permanent markers all have very distinctive smells, but be careful that they are not overpowering.

Lay these out and ask the children to identify smells that they like or that they don't like. Provide them with a set of happy and sad stickers. Ask the children to place a sad sticker on items they don't like the smell of and a happy one on those they do. Don't allow the child to smell any toxins and only allow the child to smell in short bursts.

For younger children, identify how they like or dislike smells through their behaviour. Familiar smells can be used to help younger children calm down, for example, a teddy washed in a particular soap brand or sprayed with the same deodorant that Mum uses.

Evoke memories through smell

Smell can be very evocative. Think back to your own childhood. What smells can you remember? Perhaps school dinners or a particular disinfectant? Maybe the library or the dentist? It may have been the smell of a match striking or gas from a cooker or fire.

Ask children what smells they can remember and chat to them about their memories. Be aware of this activity, as some memories are hard, such as a hospital visit or flowers at a funeral. Some may be happy ones, such as visits to the seaside or the local park. Ask the children to tell you about 'happy' or 'sad' smells.

Story smells
Equipment
story book or make up a story with children/various items associated with story/cardboard box

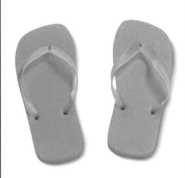

Activity and story smells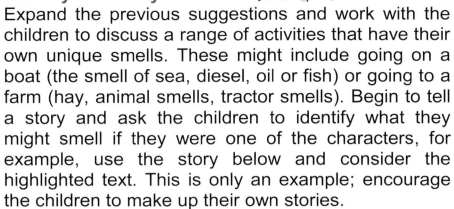

Expand the previous suggestions and work with the children to discuss a range of activities that have their own unique smells. These might include going on a boat (the smell of sea, diesel, oil or fish) or going to a farm (hay, animal smells, tractor smells). Begin to tell a story and ask the children to identify what they might smell if they were one of the characters, for example, use the story below and consider the highlighted text. This is only an example; encourage the children to make up their own stories.

Extend this activity by creating a 'smell box' of items so that the children can smell, touch and see the items included in a story. Work with the children's own interests and experiences.

Jennifer was excited. She was going on holiday and Mum had asked her to pack a case of the things she needed to take.

She looked in her cupboard and decided to pack her **flip-flops** for the beach. She also needed some **sun cream** in case it was hot. Jenny enjoyed reading and made sure she packed a good **book**. She also liked to draw and colour, so she took out some **paper, felt pens and pencils**. She made sure she had a **rubber** to put in her pencil case too.

Mum had washed her **clothes**, and she chose what she wanted from the washing pile.

Dad called out that he wanted to pack the car, and at the last moment Jenny picked up her sunglasses and **leather purse** and ran outside.

Before they went on holiday, Dad always mowed the lawn so that the **grass** would not be too long when they returned. Jenny ran across the lawn with her case and handed it to her dad. They all got in the car, Mum and Dad in the front, Jenny and her **dog**, Gunner, in the back. Gunner's **dog food** was in a big sack under Jenny's feet. Dad started the car and they began their long journey to the sea…

Using heat to enhance smells

Smells are often stronger when enhanced by heat sources. A scented candle has little smell before being lit but once alight gives off a strong aroma. Think about what you can use to enhance smells through a heat source. Some of your ideas may include cooking, such as smelling coffee, bacon cooking or toast.

Try it with the children. Ask them to gather together a range of 'ingredients' and divide them up into small piles. Use a simple candle or tea light for the heat source. Ensure that it is safe by placing it in a suitable container such as a jam jar or use an oil burner.

If using a candle, place a small amount of the ingredients into the bowl of a metal spoon. Make sure the handle of the spoon is insulated from the heat by wrapping it in cotton wool, kitchen roll or fabric. Secure the insulation in place with tape to ensure it does not go near the flame. Adult supervision required at all times!

Heat up the ingredients on the spoon by placing it over the heat source, and consider the smells. Are they the same or different? Do the ingredients look the same or have they changed? Experiment with the children; some ingredients will work well and others will work not as well. Consider what the children have chosen, and if you feel that they are not going to achieve much with their chosen ingredients add to the pile with items such as lemon zest, coffee or herbs.

The ultimate heat source!

Bonfires! Have you ever smelled a bonfire and cooked marshmallows on sticks? The experience is memory making. If you are struggling with permission to undertake this type of activity, write your normal risk assessment and also write down the benefits of the activity for the child or young person. Sell the activity on the benefits; they will probably outweigh the risks!

Smell and epilepsy

Primrose is a happy girl attending a local primary school. She enjoys being with others and playing. She happens to have epilepsy, and all staff members are vigilant when watching her as her seizures vary from small absences through to tonic-clonic seizures (also known as grand mal seizures).

One of the specific indicators that Primrose is going into a seizure is when she starts to sniff the air. She is unable to explain what she smells but tells you that it is a nasty smell. This is only for a few seconds before she starts her seizure. Her teaching assistant needs to be aware so that she can lower her to the floor and move furniture away to give her a safe place.

Aversion to smells

In the same class is a young gentleman called Baha. He happens to be on the autism spectrum and is very gifted in particular areas, specifically with numbers.

Baha is hypersensitive to smells. He has a teaching assistant, who is employed to work on a one-to-one basis with him for several hours each day. Baha gets on well with other students and his class teacher but reacts strongly when his teaching assistant sits too close. He becomes violent, hits out and runs away.

Initially, it was thought that the response was around personal space, but Baha was happy to sit next to his class teacher. After careful consideration, it was discovered that Baha had an aversion to the smell of the particular deodorant worn by his teaching assistant.

She replaced it with the same brand used by both his mum and class teacher. This was familiar to him and a smell he could cope with. Immediately, it changed his response. The incident helped the school to appreciate some of Baha's other behavioural traits related specifically to this hypersensitivity.

Chapter Seven
Creating sensory play:
Playing with balance

Balance is very different for each of us: some find it easy to walk and step up and down kerbs; some find this simple activity extremely difficult; and others find that normal activities are not enough and wish to explore and extend their balance into gymnastics or extreme activities such as free running.

The activities suggested in this chapter are ones that can take place at home or in your setting with a little preparation. They are designed to be fun and allow the child to explore their own abilities. Encourage the child to participate, be aware of their specific needs and be available but try not to take over or make decisions for them.

Jason happens to have dyspraxia. This means that he finds balance and coordination difficult. He also has difficulty in processing the world around him and needs additional time for instructions to sink in, and prefers instructions to be clear and easy to understand. Jason is a visual and kinetic learner so will respond better if shown photographs or symbols to illustrate instruction.

Over time, Jason has had many different hospital appointments and trips to A&E for various injuries caused by him simply being clumsy. His mum has become paranoid about his participation in anything she deems risky, including simple balancing games. She has asked the setting to ensure that he is not included in anything that will be dangerous. Jason wants to be the same as all the other children and needs to be given the same choices.

Within this chapter, consider how you could ensure Jason is included.

Balancing with balloons

Balancing games do not necessarily need the child to be standing. These games encourage the children to roll around and have fun while learning how to control their bodies and adapt their postures to balance and to coordinate their limbs.

Start off by blowing up at least 30 balloons. Alter the pressure in the balloons by blowing some up full and others half full. Add different size and shape balloons.

Place the balloons in a confined play area such as a play tent, paddling pool or large cardboard box. There is no aim to this activity apart from having fun. Encourage the children to roll around on the balloons and have fun.

Be aware of children who dislike the feel of rubber or the smell of balloons or who fear the sound of a balloon bursting. Some children may like to play this game wearing ear defenders.

For children who are particularly anxious about playing, blow the balloons up so that they are semi-inflated. Feed them into a duvet cover and let the children play on top of it.

Having half-inflated balloons will mean that the game lasts longer; being inside the duvet cover they will be contained and the child will not see or feel the rubber balloons. If any of the balloons burst, the noise will be deadened slightly by being enclosed.

Extension activity for outside

Create your own water bed by half inflating balloons using water, and place inside a duvet cover. Play with it on the grass. Even very young children enjoy this activity. Challenge the children to walk or crawl across the duvet cover. Try to have races across the duvet cover or crawl underneath it. Allow the children freedom to explore this sensory experience.

Creating a balance machine

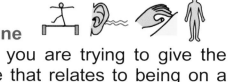

This activity is excellent if you are trying to give the child a sensory experience that relates to being on a boat. It is accessible to all ages with a little help and support.

Use an old tray (metal is preferable) or a large wooden cutting board. Place a line of large round stones on flat ground and place the board on top. Support the child to either sit or stand on the board and rock from side to side, 'balancing' on the stones. Experiment with varying difficulty. The hardest balance is when there is only one large round stone beneath the board and it can lean in any direction. Expand this by balancing the board on a small or large ball.

Balancing on objects

Encourage the child to initially play with the stones and try to balance them one on top of the other. Can they then balance other objects on top of the stones?

Make sure the stones are smooth with no sharp edges. Create a series of stepping stones and see if the child can balance by walking across the stones. Try other objects to walk on and see if it is easy or hard. If the child is young, try placing sturdy plastic mugs upside down on the floor to walk across. If the child is having difficulty, look at how you can simplify the activity for them such as stomping across cushions laid out on the floor.

Expand this game by walking across different surfaces. Use the ideas for textured floor surfaces mentioned in Chapter Two. Ask the children to make their way across the room using just two of the surfaces. They have to balance their way and help each other in pairs.

Balancing on tins or pieces of wood

This is an old favourite but still holds attraction for children. Wash out two matching food tins. Punch a hole in each side and thread through heavy string or lightweight rope to create a pair of simple stilts. This activity can also be done with pieces of wood.

83

Balancing on balls

Gather together a whole range of different sized balls from a tennis ball size up to a giant exercise ball size; whatever you are able to access.

Play with the children by asking them to sit on the ball with their feet on the ground. After a count of three, children lift their feet and see how long they can balance without touching the ground. Supervise this activity and be aware of children potentially hurting themselves.

Play this game and ask the child to balance on their tummy, back, feet or other part of their body. This kind of activity is often used by occupational therapists and physiotherapists.

Making your own balance beam

Plenty of balance beams are available to purchase. If you are making your own, be aware of the safety issues and ensure the beam is secure.

In the illustration we have used a simple scaffold board and some pieces of railway sleeper. We recognise that not all settings have these items to hand, but it is possible to create your own with what you have available. We encouraged the children to 'walk the plank' and enhanced the experience by providing a blue plastic sheet to represent the sea.

Look for what is available to you in your setting or around the home. Make it exciting for the children so that they want to participate. If you have the opportunity, take children to the local park. There will be plenty of equipment that will encourage them to balance. Note that the image on the right shows Nyasha and Rutendo playing in the park in the dark. This has

made it a special, exciting and memorable sensory experience. Remember to take a torch.

Illustration shows the
response to the instruction
'no limbs on the ground'

No limbs on the ground
Another version of this
game uses sheets of
newspaper laid on the
ground. When the leader
calls out, the group must all
be on the newspaper with
no limbs touching the floor.

After the first go, the sheet
of newspaper gets folded in
half. Each time the paper
gets smaller it is more
difficult for everyone to stay
on the sheet and therefore
requires balance,
coordination and
cooperation to play the
game in a team.

**The Leaning Tower of
Pisa**
This is a game for three
people. Stand next to each
other and interlock arms.
The centre person is the
tower and each person on
the sides leans outwards as
far as they feel comfortable.
The winner is the group
who stayed upright the
longest.

Balancing games

Out on a limb

Children love the opportunity to play this game; it always evokes lots of laughter. Adapt the game depending on the ages of the children participating, keeping it simple for younger children by only using feet.

Each child has an opportunity to use face or body paints to paint a different colour on to the top of each foot and back of their hands. Each child should have four colours.

The leader (an adult or a child) shouts out two, three or four colours, for example, blue, red and green. The children put the correct colour painted hand(s) or foot/feet on the ground but can only use those colours called out. Therefore, they need to balance using the correct limb.

The game does not necessarily require body paints to be used. Simply call out different instructions for them to follow such as three feet and three hands (as illustrated) or two bottoms, three feet and two hands.

The game is fun and the children help each other. Challenge: Think about how you can adapt this game if you are working with children who have restricted movement or are wheelchair users.

85

1,2,3 Sit!
Equipment **P+**
none/
last person stands near to a
wall or fence

1,2,3 Stand!
Equipment
none

1,2,3 Sit! Play this game with primary age and older children. Ask the children to all stand in a line facing front to back. Have a little space between each one (less than an arm's length away). On the command '1,2,3 Sit!' all the children sit on the lap of the child behind. Either all the children will balance and have their own seat or one will start to rock and the whole row falls over. This game works best if the last person in the line leans against a wall or fence.

1,2,3 Stand! Ask a group of four or more children to sit in a circle either facing inwards or outwards. They interlock arms. On the count of '1,2,3 Stand!' the children all need to stand up but without touching the floor with their hands; they can only help each other. It is fun if the group is made up of six or seven children.

A salutary tale…

Jessica is 4 years old. Every day, she walks to school with her mummy. During the journey, they pass a small retaining wall just two feet high. Jessica sees the other children walking on the wall. Each day she asks, "Can I walk on the wall?" but her mother says, "No, you will fall off and hurt yourself." Eventually, Jessica hears this so often that she is conditioned into believing she cannot undertake this task.

At school, her teacher is practising with the balance beam, encouraging children to participate. When it is Jessica's turn, she says, "No, I will fall off and hurt myself." No persuasion makes any difference. She is unable to undertake the task as she has been conditioned not to.

The school support her to participate. Initially, she walks along a length of string on the floor. Next, she is given the balance beam but with no legs; just a board on the floor. Again, she is able to participate. Eventually, she walks the beam with support from two staff members. Her self-esteem and confidence increase; she is very proud of herself.

Challenge: Do we limit children's abilities through our own fears and anxieties?

86

EY   P+

Consider how you would adapt the activities to be suitable for all ages. Think creatively and decide how the sensory experience can still be achieved even if the child is unable to participate.

Body awareness is all about knowing where your body is, how it is moving and how it relates to things around it and other people.

The sensory play activities described in this chapter encourage children to use their bodies and to recognise the feelings of proximity to others and objects. Some children may need a little more help than others as well as reassurance that is it okay to participate.

We have also added some games and activities where the children need to identify where they are in relation to a space or place. Other activities play with pressure or touch against the body such as the image of Rutendo in the ball pool.

Remember the story in Chapter One of Jhasinda, who hated light touch? Stroking her skin was painful for her, but being wrapped tightly in a blanket was comforting. Children will respond in different ways to these activities.

Be aware of children who are hyposensitive to body awareness: some may not understand personal space, standing too close for comfort; some may constantly bump into objects or misjudge distances or have difficulty with fine motor skills.

As we advocate throughout the book, take a person-centred approach to these activities. Think of things from the child's perspective. What do you need to do to ensure that the child can participate? Also remember that touch of any description may be inappropriate due to cultural or religious grounds. Encourage children to participate but don't push them into activities that they are uncomfortable with.

87

Spatial awareness game

Find an open space or empty room such as a sports hall. Work with the children to get their bearings. Take a look around the area and point out various features.

Ask the children to get into small groups of four children. Identify the group by a name. Now blindfold each child. Turn each child around several times and send them off to walk in different directions.

The aim of the game is for each group of children to find each other. They do this by calling out the name of the group and listening for this above the rest of the children calling out.

The game causes children to bump into one another. When they do, they must say the name of their group to see if they have found another member. If not, they move on. The winners are the first group to re-form.

Extension activities
To make this more fun, give each group an animal name. The groups find each other by making the sound of the animal their group is named after.

Why not try a game with no sound, but the children identify group members through touch, for example, each child in a group carries the same tactile object such as fur fabric or shiny paper. The children need to recognise if it is the same as theirs.

Health & Safety: keep all areas clear of furniture or tripping hazards. Make sure there is plenty of supervision. Children who do not want to participate in the game can become helpers and watchers, supporting others who wander away from the action.

Challenge: What other games can you think of that use blindfolds to support other sensory experiences? Consider taste, hearing, touch and balance.

For younger children, play with a blindfold and encourage the child to find your hand, foot, nose or hair by feel.

Wrapping up a parcel
Equipment
various wrapping
materials/floor space

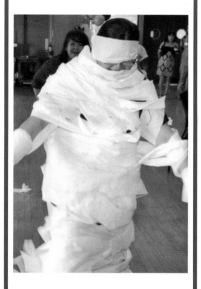

Wrapping up a parcel

This simple game involves wrapping a child up as a parcel. Various things can be used as the wrapping such as bubble wrap, tissue paper, wrapping paper, wallpaper, toilet roll, towels and blankets or a rug.

Encourage the children to roll around on the floor and feel the sensation of being wrapped up. Bubble wrap is particularly good and even more fun if the children can burst the bubbles. Beware of suffocation.

Hula hoop games

Hula hoops are very versatile. Weighted hoops can be purchased easily and are not expensive. Some children will prefer this type of hoop to play with.

Hula spin

Two children climb inside the same hula hoop. They spin around as fast as they can, each holding on to the hoop. The children need to be aware of their own body and that of the second child. The children will become dizzy and will need a little time to reorient themselves after the activity.

Hula jumps

Place a number of hoops on the ground. Ask the child to hop, skip or jump into each hoop. While they are in the hoop, ask them to do an action such as to close their eyes and touch their nose, or to do a handstand.

Hula potted sports

There are many movements that can be done with hula hoops such as climbing through them, rolling them, putting them over heads, spinning them on arms and waists and jumping in and out of them. Work with the children to develop several activities and play team games, with each child copying the movement of the previous child.

Ask the children to stand in a row or circle, each holding hands. This works best with at least six children. The first child has a hula hoop, and without losing hand contact with the next person the hoop must travel down the row or around the circle with everyone going through it. This involves body awareness and balance.

Obstacle races and assault courses
Equipment
various items from around the setting such as ropes, balloons, netting, fabric, balance beams and cardboard boxes

Finding your way

Obstacle races and assault courses are good for body awareness. Children need to recognise where they are in relation to obstacles and also recognise what they need to do to get around, through, under or over them. Ask the children to help you find items around the setting that would be good to add to an obstacle race or visit a local park that has an assault course. Don't forget the value of climbing rocks and trees.

Hanging balloon bags
This idea is slightly different. Fill a number of balloons with a little water, blow them up and hang them from the rafters or an outside pergola (the water adds a little weight). The children negotiate their way through the balloon maze, trying not to touch them. If the child touches a balloon, they need to retrace their steps and start from the beginning again.

Try pinning balloons to a wall or large noticeboard. Play a game with several children where the left hand has to touch a yellow balloon, the right hand a green balloon, etc. The children have to think about where their body is and, if playing with several children, need to consider where their body is in relation to others.

Amber happens to have dyspraxia and autism. She has difficulty in understanding spatial awareness and will not recognise when she is too close to others. However, she does not like people being too close to her.

Her parents taught her that it was not socially acceptable to stand too close to another person and that she would have a better response from others if she stood an arm's length away to have a conversation.

They practised the spacing by playing the 'arm game', standing next to each other but creating the space by measuring an arm's length. Amber got used to standing an arm's length away from others and found life was much easier when people did not back away from her all the time when she stood next to them.

90

Chapter Nine
The sensory story challenge

Consider the short story below and think back through the ideas in this book. Pick out elements in the story and think about how you can use them to create sensory experiences for children and young people using everyday resources. Don't limit yourself to this story; take a look at other books, new and old favourites. How can you make opportunities for children to participate in new and exciting ways?

The friend's adventure

"Hey, Jack," whispered Evan, "I can see a ghost." "Where?" responded Jack, pointing his torch into the blackness.

The two boys were camping in the garden. They had made their own tent from a large sheet hung over a rope, which was tied between two trees. The ground was lumpy and bumpy but they had created a fantastic soft den using lots of duvets, sleeping bags, pillows and cushions.

It was dark, the evening air was damp and the grass outside the tent was wet to touch. Earlier in the evening, they had had a fire and the embers were still glowing red.

"Over there. Look!" whispered Evan, pointing up into a tree. "Through the branches. See! It's moving." Jack looked up to where Evan was pointing. Sure enough, he did see something white and misty. It seemed to be floating on a branch.

"I'm going to investigate," said Evan, stepping out of the tent. "Aargh, it's wet out here," he said as his bare feet touched the wet grass. Jack handed Evan the torch; he did not want to go outside. An owl hooted as Jack crept back inside the tent. "Did you hear that?" said Evan. "I think it was the ghost."

Both boys stood still listening to the evening sounds. Every time they heard a sound Evan shone the torch to see what it was. The torch light reflected on the wet grass.

They both froze; a long howl came from a tree branch. The boys were scared. Could it be the ghost? Evan shone the torch in the direction of the tree, slowly lighting up the trunk. They could see the dark bark, the shadow of green leaves and, as the torchlight moved upwards, they saw a long, swaying white ribbon.

Was it the ghost? Slowly, Evan moved the torch; the beam travelled further up the branch following the ribbon. The boys saw it wasn't a ribbon at all; it was a tail. They had found their ghost. It was Snowball the cat sitting on a branch howling at the moon!

91

Creating sensory activities from the story

The following are only suggestions for sensory activities relating to the story. The challenge is up to you to encourage the children's imagination and creativity in order to support sensory experiences.

- Make dens from sheets, rope or cardboard boxes
- Fill the den with different surfaces to represent 'lumps and bumps'
- Add lots of soft furnishings and bedding to create a cosy nest
- Turn the lights off in a room and block out light from the windows
- Play with torches and coloured filters to light up parts of the room
- Build a pretend fire with twigs. Place some battery-powered tea lights between the sticks and cover with a lightweight red fabric to represent the embers
- Create a wet touch activity to represent wet grass. Allow the children to experience this sensation barefooted
- Listen to various night-time sounds. Recreate those sounds using everyday items
- Create an activity using torchlight and reflection. Shine a torch on your own face while looking in a mirror
- Play a game of ghosts where the children become ghosts using sheets and blankets
- Gather together a range of natural items to feel and smell, such as bark, leaves, grass and flowers
- Slide pieces of ribbon (wet and dry) across bare skin
- Play a game of being a cat: the sounds they make; the movements they make. Enhance this by asking the children to feel fur fabric
- Create cat masks and play hide-and-seek in the dark. The cat hides and the children find it

These are just some ideas. Consider what else you could do to create sensory experiences for the children.

Quick ideas sensory play activity sheets

In the next chapter we offer some quick ideas sensory play activity sheets. Copy these and give them to families to undertake at home. Each sheet contains simple ideas using everyday items found around the house. We have found that many parents are interested in playing with their children but lack the ideas to do so. Try making your own ideas sheets and simple sensory bags using everyday items.

We have not specifically focused on any one sense in the activity sheets; many ideas provide experiences for more than one sense. We have used the same visual key used in this book to show what senses are used for each activity.

All the resources in this section are free to photocopy and use. Enlarge each resource on a photocopier as appropriate.

1. Activity diary template (page 16)

Draw a picture or paste on a photo of your activity

©www.theplaydoctors.co.uk

Name and date:

How did the activity make you feel?

Notes to share:

2. All about me communication passports template 1 (page 20)

These are very simple templates, but they are useful when the child is going to a new setting or is meeting people for the first time. Complete the details, print, cut out and laminate. Keep in your wallet and use as appropriate

Front

Back

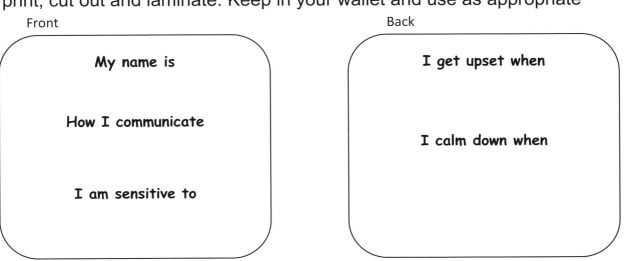

My name is

How I communicate

I am sensitive to

I get upset when

I calm down when

3. All about me communication passport template 2 (page 20)

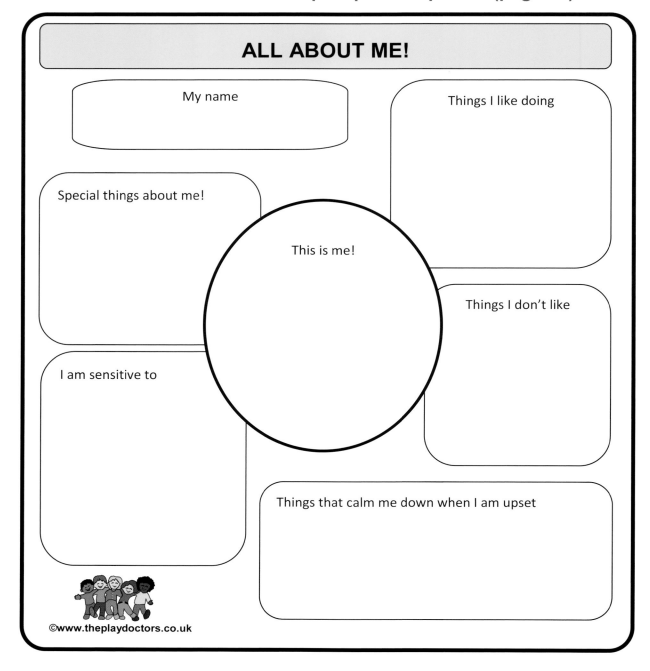

ALL ABOUT ME!

My name

Things I like doing

Special things about me!

This is me!

Things I don't like

I am sensitive to

Things that calm me down when I am upset

©www.theplaydoctors.co.uk

4. Noise-O-Meter and emotions template (page 55)

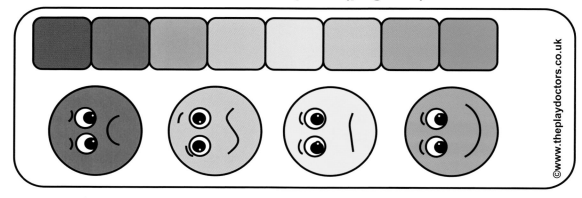

©www.theplaydoctors.co.uk

Five minute sensory play activity cards

Kitchen music **Sensory Play Sheet 1**

Take a look in your cupboards and find items for children to make music. Ideas include:
- Banging wooden spoons on saucepans
- Shaking containers filled with rice or pasta
- Use a teaspoon to gently tap drinking glasses filled with different levels of water
- Running the end of a spoon over the outside of a colander or grater

What else can you use?

Painting with diamonds **Sensory Play Sheet 2**

Purchase a packet of Epsom salts or sea salt (granular not powdered). Mix a teaspoon of salt with some water-based paint and add a little extra water. Stir well. Paint on to a thick paper using a large brush.

The salt crystals will be picked up in the paint, and when the picture is dry it will shine like diamonds! Try creating diamond butterflies by dabbing colour on to one side of the paper and folding it over to create a matching print. Use shiny stickers to create the body and head.

What else can you paint?

Create a miniature garden  **Sensory Play Sheet 3**

Find a plastic tray or container. Fill it with sand or rice to create a surface to 'plant' various items. Take a look around the kitchen or outside. What is available to plant or decorate the garden with? What about using:
- A plastic bottle top to create a miniature pond (fill with water). Add bits of carrot to create fish
- A piece of cauliflower or broccoli to create trees
- Breakfast cereal (various) to create pathways or flowers
- Herbs to create green grass

What else can you use?

Sensory taste tubs    Sensory Play Sheet 4

Find about ten plastic tubs or containers. Take a look around and find different safe textured foods to put into the tubs. Consider powder, liquid, loose foods and sticky stuff. Allow the children to feel, smell and taste the tubs. What about using:

- Sugar, powdered milk, powered custard, coffee granules, flour
- Sultanas, small breakfast cereal, frozen peas or sweetcorn
- Pieces of jelly, jam, peanut butter (beware of allergies), honey or syrup
- Milk, fruit juice, water, fizzy drinks

What else can you use?

Shaving foam fun  Sensory Play Sheet 5

A simple but brilliant activity to do in the bath – it washes straight off!
Place a large plastic dustbin liner in the bottom of the bath. Support children to squirt two or three cans of shaving foam into the bag. Fold over the top and tape closed. Allow the children to create a series of small holes in the bag using the sharp end of a pencil or scissors (supervised). Get them to climb into the bath and manipulate the bag creating small shaving foam worms. Play until the shaving foam is all out of the bag. Slide up and down the bath and have fun. Add some drops of food colouring into the foam to create colours.
Use the foam to draw on to the sides of the bath and any tiles.

What about doing this outside on a plastic sheet?

Sensory baths Ideas   Sensory Play Sheet 6

Simply fill twenty or so balloons with warm water as you are filling the bath. Add lots of bubbles to the bath so that the bottom of the bath cannot be seen. Drop the balloons into the water and allow the children to get in and feel the squashy balloons beneath the water. Add a pile of coloured ice cubes to the bath water. They will float and eventually melt. Try mixing natural food colouring with sea salt and let it dry. Put it into the bath to colour the water and add a grainy texture. Try adding a packet of powder drink mix to colour and scent the water, or perhaps play with raw jelly cubes until they dissolve.

What else can you think of to make bath time fun?

Sensory play does not have to cost the earth. It just takes a little imagination and a sense of freedom to create unique sensory experiences that the child will always remember. Have fun!